ASTROLOGY & HOROSCOPES

ASTROLOGY & HOROSCOPES

GEDDES & GROSSET

Contents

Introduction

History

Astrology is an ancient craft that has its origin in the mists of time. It is impossible to place accurately the beginnings, but one thing that is certain is that astrology began as a subject intimately combined with astronomy. Its history is therefore the history of astronomy until the two subjects parted company, a split that essentially began when Nicolai Copernicus (1473–1543) published his book *De revolutionibus*. In this book he postulated that, contrary to earlier thinking in which the earth was the centre of the solar system, the Sun actually formed the focus about which all the planets orbited.

It is thought that there was some study of these subjects five to six thousand years ago when Chaldean priests made maps of the skies. The Chaldeans were the most ancient of the Babylonian peoples. It was believed that heavenly bodies exerted influence upon man and whatever could not be ascribed to man must be due to actions of the gods or the deities of the planets. Subsequent study of the solar system began as pure observation because records and other data for calculation simply did not exist. The Egyptian and Greek civilizations gave much to the theories and practice of astrology, although much remained unwritten. It is said that the Chaldeans instructed the priests of the Pharaohs in astrology, and monuments exist that show a working knowledge of the subject. This was around 400–350 BC. A little earlier, in Greece around the beginning of the sixth century BC, the philosopher Thales (*c*.643–*c*.546 BC) studied astronomy and astrology as did Pythagoras (569–470 BC) who was credited by Copernicus as the person who developed the theory that the earth and other planets revolved around the Sun.

There were many other Greek students, notably: Plato; Hippocrates, who combined astrology with medical diagnosis; Hipparchus, the founder of observational astronomy, who in 134 BC discovered a new star; and Claudius Ptolemaeus (100–178 AD). Ptolemy wrote the *Almagest*, which is a star catalogue of just over a thousand stars, and also a consideration of the motion of the Moon and the planets. He also wrote the *Tetrabiblos*, the earliest surviving book on astrology.

In Rome and the extended empire at this time, astrology was held in very high regard, and great faith was placed in the work and advice of astrologers who were appointed to the Emperors. The Moon was considered particularly influential and can be found depicted on many of their coins. Among the many Romans active in this field were Porphyry (232–304 AD), who is said to have developed the house method, and Julius Maternus (around 300 AD), who wrote a number of books on astrology.

From about 500 AD Arabs became the prime movers in science and philosophy, but by the early Middle Ages (the thirteenth century) interest was rekindled in Europe, at which time astrology had been divided into three distinct fields: *natural* or *mundane* astrology, which is prominent in forecasting national events, weather, etc; *horary* astrology, used to answer a question through the use of a chart drawn up for the actual time of asking; and *judicial* astrology, in which the fortune of an individual is determined by using a birth chart.

The fifteenth and sixteenth centuries in Europe saw the rise of several famous names, including the Polish astronomer Copernicus. Although Copernicus concurred with the views of Pythagoras, he could not prove the theory, and many attribute the real establishment of the principle (i.e. that the planets orbit the Sun) to Johannes Kepler (1571–1630), the German astronomer. The medieval precursor of chemistry was alchemy, and one famous practitioner was Phillipus Aureolus Paracelsus (1493–1541), who also had some astrological leanings. He believed that the Sun, planets and stars influenced people, whether for good or evil. From this era also came Nostradamus (1503–1566). Michael Nostradamus has become one of the most famous of astrologists and prophets, and he also studied medicine. Almost from the outset it was thought that medical knowledge must, by necessity, include an understanding of astrology.

The work of the Dane Tycho Brahe (1546–1601) could, in some respects, be considered a watershed in the study of astrology/astronomy. Brahe became an observer of the heavens and in so doing was recognized as the most accurate since Hipparchus, centuries before. He prepared tables, designed instruments and studied the motion of the planets, particularly Mars, and it was this initial work that led Kepler to formulate his famous laws of planetary motion. Kepler was assistant to Brahe when the latter moved to Prague following the death of his patron, King Frederick. Kepler's work proved to be pivotal in advancing the understanding of astronomy. Kepler compared the work of Ptolemy, Copernicus and Tycho Brahe to produce three laws:

1 The orbit of each planet is an ellipse with the Sun at one of the foci (an ellipse has two foci.)

2 A line drawn from a planet to the Sun sweeps out equal areas in equal times.

3 The squares of the sidereal periods (time taken to orbit the Sun, measured relative to the stars) are proportional to the cubes of the mean distances from the Sun.

Kepler believed that the stars exerted an influence upon

events and that astrology could predict the most mundane of happenings. During the sixteenth and seventeenth centuries there were many famous names who combined astrology with astronomy, mathematics or, commonly, medicine. These included the Italian physicist Galileo Galilei, a French professor of mathematics and doctor of medicine, Jean Morin, an Italian monk and mathematician, Placidus de Tito, and in England, William Lilly, who became famous as a practitioner of horary astrology and accurately predicted the Great Fire of London in 1666.

The poet John Dryden used astrology in predicting numerous events in his own life and the lives of his sons, including both their deaths. Following Dryden's own death in 1700, although not because of it, astrological practice declined on the continent but flourished in England. This influence extended to France at the start of the nineteenth century, where a sound scientific basis to the subject was sought.

William Allan (1800–1917), otherwise known as Alan Leo, was considered by many to be the father of modern astrology. He lectured widely throughout England and edited a magazine called *Modern Astrology*. He was also a professional astrologer and a prolific author on the subject, writing 30 books. In 1915 he founded the Astrological Lodge of London. Although the war years were disruptive to the study and practice of astrology, a large following was developed in North America. However, continental Europe suffered during the Second World War as Hitler's forces caused wholesale destruction, and Hitler himself, unhappy with adverse astrological predictions, destroyed books and records and incarcerated unfortunate practitioners.

Today astrology holds interest for many people, and growing numbers are becoming fascinated by its study. However, there is a dichotomy between astrology and astronomy.

The Solar System

The early visualizations of the heavens and the stars showed the Earth at the centre of a large revolving sphere. It was thought that the stars seen in the sky were somehow fastened onto the inner surface of this sphere. The stars that appeared to revolve around the Earth but did not move in relation to each other were called the 'fixed stars'. Among the many fixed stars there are some in particular that have certain characteristics and that can be used in astrological charts. For example, Regulus (or Alpha Leonis) is the brightest star in the constellation of Leo and signifies pride, good luck and success.

From early times it was noted that while many stars remained fixed, five in particular did not, and these wandered about the sky. These were the planets of the solar system because at that time not all eight remaining planets (other than Earth) had been identified. The discovery of Uranus, Neptune and Pluto followed the invention of the telescope, and Uranus was the first planet so observed, in 1781.

For the purposes of astrology, the Sun, which is actually a star, is considered as a planet. It is approximately 150 million kilometres from Earth and has a diameter of 1.4 million kilometres. Energy is generated in the core, from nuclear fusion, where the temperature is about fifteen million degrees.

The planets

The Moon is a satellite of Earth but for convenience is also treated as a planet. It orbits the Earth roughly every 27 days, and the same face is always kept towards Earth, lit by light reflected from the Sun. The Moon seems to change size—the process known as waxing and waning—and it is called 'new' when it is situated between the Earth and the Sun and, because it is not illuminated, cannot be seen. The full Moon occurs about 14 days later, when the full face is totally illuminated.

Planets with their orbits between the Sun and the Earth's orbit are called 'inferior'. There are two planets in this category, Mercury and Venus. Mercury is the smallest planet in the solar system and takes 88 Earth days to complete one orbit, rotating slowly on its axis, and taking 58 Earth days for one revolution. Its elliptical orbit is eccentric, varying in distance from the Sun from 47 to 70 million kilometres.

Venus is the brightest planet seen from Earth and is known as the morning or evening star. It is about 108 million kilometres from the Sun and has a diameter similar to Earth's, at 12,300 kilometres. Venus spins very slowly on its axis, and a day is equivalent to 24.3 Earth days, and a year is 225 days. It is unusual in being the only planet to revolve in the opposite direction to the path of its orbit.

The remaining planets, from Mars to Pluto, are called the 'superior planets', being on the distant side of Earth from the Sun. Mars takes about 687 Earth days to complete an orbit, and a day is just a fraction longer than one Earth day. The surface is solid and mainly red in colour because of the type of rock. There are many surface features, some of which are attributed to the action of water, although none is found there now. Mars is sometimes a dominant feature of the night sky, particularly when it occasionally approaches nearer to Earth, and it has from ancient times exerted considerable fascination.

Jupiter is the largest and heaviest planet in the solar system and has a diameter of 142,800 kilometres. The planet gives out more energy than it receives from the Sun and must therefore have an internal energy source. It is due, in part, to this that the atmosphere is seen to be in steady movement. Parallel bands of colour are seen, but a particularly noticeable feature is the Great Red Spot, which is thought to be an enormous storm, larger than Earth, coloured red because of the presence of phosphorus. The magnetic field of Jupiter is thousands of times stronger than Earth's, and radio waves emanate from the planet. Jupiter has 18 satellites, or moons, of which four are called the 'Galilean satellites'—Io, Europa, Ganymede and Callisto—because they were first seen by Galileo in 1610. There are three other groups of satellites, of which the innermost contains Adastrea, Amalthea, Metis and Thebe.

The next planet out from the Sun is Saturn, the second largest in the solar system. It has a diameter of 120,800 kilometres and the orbit takes 29 Earth years at a distance of 1507 million kilometres from the Sun. Because of its rapid rotation, Saturn is flattened at the poles with a consequent bulging at its equator. A day lasts for a little over 10 hours, and the surface temperature is -170 degrees Celsius. The most obvious and interesting feature of Saturn is its rings, which consist of ice, dust and rock debris, and some of which may have derived from the break-up of a satellite. The rings are about a quarter of a million kilometres across, and there are three main ones but hundreds of smaller ones.

Saturn also has 24 satellites, or moons, of which Titan is the largest with a diameter of 5200 kilometres (larger than Mercury). Some moons were discovered by the Voyager spacecraft in 1989, including Atlas, Calypso and Prometheus.

The planets Mercury through to Saturn were all known to astrologers and astronomers for many years. The remaining planets, Uranus, Neptune and Pluto, were discovered only in modern times, after the advent of the telescope. These are therefore often called the 'modern planets' by astrologers.

Uranus is 50,080 kilometres in diameter and a day lasts

17 hours while a year is equivalent to 84 Earth years. Because of its tilted axis, some parts of the planet's surface are in light for about 40 years and then in darkness for the remainder of its year. Uranus was discovered by William Herschel in 1781 but was something of a mystery until 1986 and the approach of Voyager. It has a faint ring system and 15 moons, some of which are very small indeed (less than 50 kilometres in diameter).

Neptune was discovered in 1846, but its existence was earlier correctly postulated because of observed irregularities in the orbit of Uranus. It takes 165 Earth years to complete an orbit and is almost 4.5 billion kilometres from the Sun. It is 17 times the mass of Earth and has a diameter at its equator of 48,600 kilometres. There are three rings and eight known satellites, the largest of which, Titan, is similar in size to the Earth's Moon.

Pluto, the smallest and most distant planet from the Sun, had its existence predicted because of its effect on the orbits of Neptune and Uranus and was finally discovered in 1930, although little is known about it. A day is equivalent to almost seven days on Earth, and a year is nearly 249 Earth years. Pluto has a very wide elliptical orbit, which brings it closest to the Sun (its *perihelion*) once in each orbit. Because of its great distance from the Sun (7.4 billion kilometres at its maximum), the surface temperature is very low, about -230 degrees Celcius. In 1979, one small moon, called Charon, was discovered, but since it is about one quarter the size of Pluto itself, the two act almost as a double planet system.

A few technicalities

As has been mentioned, the orbits of the planets are elliptical rather than circular, and there is a degree of eccentricity as well. When viewed from Earth, this combination of factors produces what may appear to be peculiar effects.

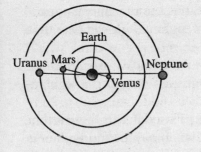

Conjunction

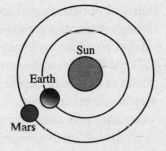

Mars in opposition to the sun

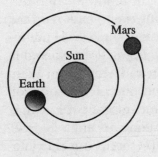

Mars in superior conjunction

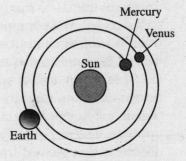

*Mercury and Venus in superior
conjunction*

Conjunctions

15

For example, planets may move around the sky, slow and then appear to move backwards for a time. This apparent backward motion is called *retrograde motion* and is simply caused by the Earth moving more quickly through its orbit in comparison to another planet. It *seems* as though the planet being observed is moving backwards, but in reality it is moving forwards, albeit in the line of sight at a slower rate. It is similar to a fast train moving alongside a slow train, which makes the latter appear to be moving backwards. In astronomical tables R denotes retrograde while D marks a return to direct motion.

Another astronomical parameter used in astrology is that of conjunctions. A *conjunction* is when two or more planets (including the Sun of course) are in a line when viewed from Earth. On occasion, Earth, Venus and the Sun will all be in a straight line. If Venus is between Earth and the Sun it is called an 'inferior conjunction'. If, however, Venus is on the other side of the Sun from Earth, it is a 'superior conjunction'. The same applies to Mercury. *Opposition* is when, for example, Earth lies between the Sun and Mars; then Mars is in opposition. Opposition is when one of the superior planets (all except Mercury, Venus and, of course, Earth) is opposite the Sun in the sky, i.e. making an angle of 180 degrees when viewed from Earth (*see* figure on previous page).

Of vital significance to the correct interpretive study of astrology are a number of parameters that enable the relative positions of planets to be fixed. These include the three great circles, one of which is the ecliptic, and the Zodiac. (A great circle is essentially any circle projected onto the celestial sphere whose plane passes through the centre of the Earth.) The horizon and celestial equator (the Earth's equator projected outward onto the celestial sphere) form two great circles, and the ecliptic is the third. The *ecliptic* is the path that the Sun apparently forms in the heavens. Of course

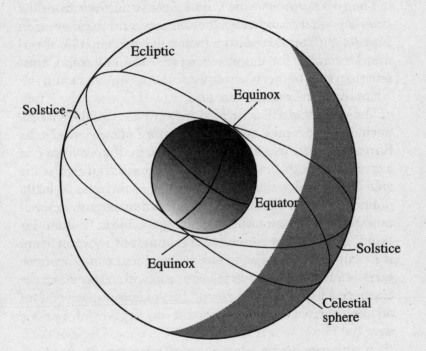

The ecliptic and the celestial sphere

the Earth orbits the Sun, but it seems from Earth to mark out a path that lies at an angle to the celestial equator. This means that the two lines cross twice, at the vernal and autumn equinoxes, otherwise known as the March equinox (or first point of the sign Aries) and September equinox (or first point of the sign Libra). (*See* figure on previous page)

The two points at which the ecliptic is farthest from the celestial equator are called the solstices, and these occur in June for the summer solstice (when the Sun enters Cancer) and December for the winter solstice (on entering Capricorn). In the southern hemisphere these equinoxes and solstices mark the reverse situation.

The ecliptic itself is divided into twelve equal divisions, each of 30 degrees, one for each of the Zodiac signs. As the Sun apparently moves around the Earth, it goes from one sign of the Zodiac to the next. A person's Sun sign is the sign before which the Sun seems to be at the time of birth.

The *Zodiac* is a 'band' in the heavens that extends to seven or eight degrees on either side of the ecliptic. Within this band, or path, are contained the apparent movements of the planets, except Pluto. The solar system can be considered as a relatively planar feature, and within this plane the Earth revolves around the Sun. The planes of the orbits of all the other planets are within seven degrees of Earth's, save for Pluto, which is nearer 17 degrees. The Zodiac is then split into twelve segments of 30 degrees, one for each sign of the Zodiac and each represented by a particular star constellation (*see* figure opposite). These signs are essentially a means of naming the sections of the sky within which the planets move. The constellation names, Scorpio, Libra, etc, have no significance although they are bound up in the development of the subject. It should be noted that today, the 30-degree segments no longer coincide with the constellation because of a phenomenon called *precession of the equinoxes*. Precession results in the Earth's axis of rotation

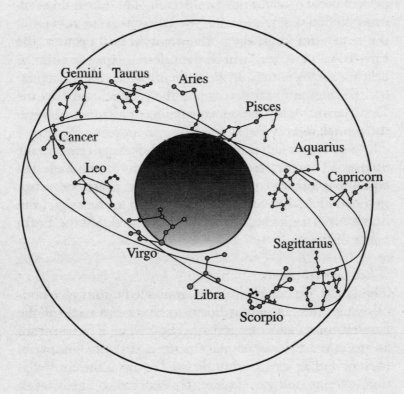

The Constellations

not remaining in the same position but forming a cone shape traced out in space. It is due to the gravitational pulls of the Sun and Moon producing a turning force, or torque. This occurs only because the Earth bulges at the equator—a perfect sphere would not be affected. The Earth takes almost 26,000 years (known as the Great Year) to sweep out the cone, and in astrology the point Aries 0 degrees (the First Point of Aries), where the celestial equator cuts the ecliptic, moves with time. Because of precession, the equator crossing-point moves around the ecliptic, and now the First Point of Aries (the vernal equinox of astronomy) lies in the constellation of Pisces and is soon to move into Aquarius. The 30 degrees along the ecliptic that is Aries remains the 30 degrees counted from the vernal equinox, although that equinox is farther back each year (this is, therefore, retrograde motion). Aries has been considered the first sign from hundreds of years BC, when it was believed that the Earth had a birthday.

The Great Year

The Great Year, as mentioned, is divided into twelve periods when the equinox is taken to be against each of the constellations that lie around the ecliptic. This is by no means an accurate division or placement, and the beginning of each period, or age, cannot be fixed easily as the constellations overlap and vary in size. However, each age is taken to be about 2000 years, and by tracing the characteristics of each age in history a pattern can be constructed. From available historical details, the last 2000 years are typified as Piscean and the 2000 years before that as Taurean. This links with the precession of the equinoxes mentioned earlier, and so the next period will be the *Age of Aquarius*.

Each age of the Great Year identified this far has certain characteristics associated with the sign. The *Age of Leo* began about 10000 BC and has as its animal representative the lion, with which are connected creativity and regality. The Sun is its planet. It is interesting to note the early attempts at art, by way of prehistoric cave paintings, and of course the vital importance of the Sun in those times.

The *Age of Cancer* (8000–6000 BC) is associated with the traits of home and family. At this time human beings began building dwellings, and some carvings symbolizing fertility have been found from this period.

From 6000 to 4000 BC was the *Age of Gemini*, which represents a sign of intellectual capacity. It is thought that writing began in some form during this Age, hence communication, a further characteristic of Gemini, became important. Civilization developed apace with cuneiform writing by the end of the Age, and it is possible that human beings had begun to travel and explore.

The *Age of Taurus* followed, from 4000 to 2000 BC, and there are numerous instances that relate to the Taurean features of solidity and security with beauty. These traits are seen in the Egyptian dynasties and the worship of the bull, and in the enormous and ornate temples and the pyramids.

The next age is that of *Aries* (2000 BC–0 AD). Aggressive and assertive qualities are associated with Aries, as are physical fitness and supremacy. These are balanced by courage and also harmony. All these characteristics are well exemplified by the Greeks, who dominated in battle and architecture and yet created the first democratic government. The symbol of the ram found an outlet in numerous ways, including as an emblem of the Roman army.

We are currently in the *Age of Pisces* (0–2000 AD), albeit towards the end of the period. It began with the birth of Christ, and there are numerous connections to the sign of the fish at this time. The secret symbol for the early Christians was the fish, Jesus was called *Ichthus*, the fish, and many of his disciples were fishermen. Qualities such as kindness, charity and forgiveness are typical, as is selflessness, although an element of confusion can also be discerned. We are on the brink of the new Age, that of *Aquarius* (2000–4000 AD), but in many respects the signs are already there to be seen. Aquarian influence can be seen in the strong presence of science and technology and space travel. Also Aquarian is a sense of detachment and of being impersonal.

Signs and Symbols

Zodiac symbols

Each sign of the Zodiac has a particular graphical represen-
tation, called a glyph, which relates to an animal or something similar. The same applies to the planets, and these symbols are used , with others, in constructing an astrological
chart.

Symbol	Sign	Representation	Name
♈	Aries	the ram's horns	The Ram
♉	Taurus	the bull's head	The Bull
♊	Gemini	two children	The Twins
♋	Cancer	the breasts	The Crab
♌	Leo	the heart, or the lion's tail	The Lion

Symbol	Sign	Representation	Name
	Virgo	the female genitalia	The Virgin
	Libra	a pair of scales	The Balance
	Scorpio	the male genitalia	The Scorpion
	Sagittarius	the Centaur's arrow	The Archer
	Capricorn	a goat's head and fish's tail	The Goat
	Aquarius	waves of water or air	The Water-bearer
H	Pisces	two fish	The Fishes

Planet symbols

The glyphs of the planets are as follows:

Planet	Symbol
Sun	☉
Moon	☽
Mercury	☿
Venus	♀
Mars	♂
Jupiter	♃
Saturn	♄
Uranus	♅
Neptune	♆
Pluto	♇

These planetary symbols are all made up of essentially the same elements, the cross, half-circle and circle, all in different combinations. These pictorial representations are linked with the very early days of human beings, when communication was achieved using such graphical methods. As such, these elements each have a particular significance:

—the circle represents eternity, something without end, the spirit;

—a dot inside a circle represents the spirit or power beginning to come out;

—the cross represents the material world;

—and the semicircle stands for the soul.

The Signs of the Zodiac

Names from the depths of history

The signs appear to have got their names from the depths of history and prehistory, and do not necessarily concur with their astronomical counterparts, the constellations. In some civilizations, the signs were attributed to parts of the body. The likeliest race to have adopted this were the Greeks, who also linked the signs to various plants.

Aries	—	the head
Libra	—	the kidneys
Taurus	—	the throat
Scorpio	—	genitalia
Gemini	—	hands and arms
Sagittarius	—	hips and thighs
Cancer	—	the breasts
Capricorn	—	the knee
Leo	—	the heart
Aquarius	—	calf and ankle
Virgo	—	the intestines
Pisces	—	the feet

Below are given the main features of the signs of the Zodiac, and these will be followed later by a fuller description of the character and personal details associated with the various sun signs, i.e. when the Sun passes through each of the signs as it appears to move on the ecliptic.

Aries

The astrological new year occurs around 21 March, when the Sun enters Aries, and this new aspect is mirrored in typical Arian traits of energy, keenness and enthusiasm. The Arian can be something of a pioneer and thus somewhat self-centred with a selfish streak. Aries is the most personal of the signs.

Taurus

Taureans seek and reflect stability, security, and are generally practical with a possessive side to their character. Risks will be taken only if they are absolutely essential, and even then it will be only after a great deal of careful thought. In general Taureans are trustworthy and pleasant and yet unenterprising, which in some may lead to them become a little boring.

Gemini

This third sign of the Zodiac is that of the heavenly twins, which, not surprisingly, can surface as a certain duality, which in a negative sense may result in someone being two-faced. Geminians are intelligent, quick of mind, versatile, and are often good communicators. If the dual nature is too strongly negative then it may lead to a lack of achievement through being over-committed and trying to do too many things at once.

Cancer

Changeable, sympathetic, kind, hard on the outside but easily hurt or offended, emotional and devoted—a home and family builder. These are all Cancerian traits and paint an essentially sensitive picture but with the strengths of devotion and faithfulness. Intellectually, Cancerians are very intuitive and have a strong imagination. If these traits are over-stressed or misused, it can lead to restlessness and over-worry.

Leo

Leo is the only sign ruled by the Sun and, like the lion, so-called king of the beasts, the Leonian can be regal, dignified and magnanimous. They are faithful, trusting but strong-willed, with fixed principles and ideas, and yet if carried too far this may result in bossiness. Similarly, someone may become snobbish, conceited and domineering.

Virgo

Virgoans are typically worker types; they dislike a leading role in anything, and yet they are intellectually very capable, although with a tendency to worry. In work and at home they pay attention to detail with precision and clarity. Closeness to others may be avoided, resulting in the perception among others of Virgoans keeping to themselves, which in turn may be misinterpreted as inhospitality.

Libra

This seventh sign of the Zodiac is opposite to Aries, which makes Librans interested in relating to a partner. As such they tend to be companionable, tactful and like to be in pleasant surroundings. Librans are often unfairly dubbed as lazy. They may also have a tendency to be quite aggressive. A Libran may be of the type who sits on the fence over an issue and, seeing both sides of an argument, may be impossibly indecisive.

Scorpio

This sign is one of intense energy, with deep, passionate feelings about the object of their attention, be it a person or an issue. Scorpions can be passionate, but in excess this can result in resentment, jealousy and even hatred. However, they can equally be warm and charming, and their virtues become apparent when dealing with real life rather than more trivial matters.

Sagittarius

In the earlier days of astrology, Sagittarius was always represented by a man joined to a horse, signifying the duality of the sign—a combination of strength and intelligence. Sagittarians are often intellectuals with a thirst for a challenge and an ability of body and mind to match. Taken to extremes, these traits can mean restlessness, carelessness, extravagance and a tendency to 'horseplay'.

Capricorn

Capricornians tend to be practical, ambitious and caring, and they often possess an excellent sense of humour. In personal relationships caution is their watchword but once decided they will make good partners. Capricornians are also traditionalists and excel in routine work or in organizational capacities. On the negative side, they may become too mean and stern, and caution may turn into selfishness.

Aquarius

Aquarians are typically independent and individualistic, and also friendly. Indeed, friendships once formed tend to be faithful, although contact with others can be rather impersonal. The freedom required by an Aquarian makes them paradoxical when it comes to love. However, the enquiring mind and originality is seen to good effect in pursuit of art or working in science and technology. An excess of Aquarian traits produces someone who is rebellious, tactless and eccentric.

Pisces

The last sign of the Zodiac, Pisces, is typified by a sensitivity that may border on the inhibited unless encouraged. Pisceans can be inspired and highly intuitive, although this may be clouded by mood swings, from elation to depression. Kindness is a common trait, and there is often a strong spiritual faith. In excess, Piscean characteristics may result in muddled thinking, weakness of character and excessive worry.

Groups of the Zodiac and Rulings

The twelve signs of the Zodiac are traditionally subdivided into a number of groups. The members of each group share certain characteristics that in terms of chart interpretation provide additional information rather than primary details.

The first grouping is the *triplicities*, otherwise known as the elements, and consists of the signs for fire, earth, air and water. Aries, Leo and Sagittarius are the *fire triplicity*. This sign is represented by a keenness and enthusiasm and a tendency literally to burn with excitement. Often more sensitive people will be considered slow and dealt with impatiently. While people with the fire sign may be lively and exuberant, their fault will often be that they are too lively. However, such tendencies are likely to be offset, to some extent, by features elsewhere in a chart.

The *earth triplicity* contains Taurus, Virgo and Capricorn and, as might be expected, people with this sign are 'down to earth', although the earth sign is not totally dominant. However, the beneficial aspects include practicality and caution, and although considered dull by livelier people, there is a reassuring solidity and trustworthiness about people with this sign.

Gemini, Libra and Aquarius form the *air triplicity*, and communication is one of the key attributes. An 'ideas person' would have this sign prominent in his or her chart, but a potential fault can be that schemes and ideas occupy too much time at the expense of productivity. In addition, such people can be dismissive of sensitivity or caution in others.

The final triplicity is that of *water*, and it contains Cancer, Scorpio and Pisces. Such people are naturally sensitive and intuitive, and often inspired, while also emotional and protective. Such people tend to be cautious of those with strong personalities, and their own faults may result from being too emotional.

It is often the case that people who have a shared strength in these signs will be compatible. Reference to the elements produces obvious attractions:

Fire — air fans the flames while water puts them out and earth smothers them.

Earth — water refreshes it while air and fire dry it out.

Air — fire responds to air, while earth and water restrict it.

Water — earth holds it, but air and fire diminish it.

The *quadruplicities* (otherwise known as qualities) form the second grouping. In this case the signs of the Zodiac are divided into three groups of four. The three qualities are 'cardinal', 'fixed' and 'mutable'. Aries, Libra, Cancer and Capricorn are of the *cardinal quadruplicity*. People with this sign dominant in their chart are outgoing and tend to lead. Taurus, Scorpio, Leo and Aquarius are of the *fixed quadruplicity*, which implies stability and a resistance to change. The *mutable quadruplicity* includes the remaining signs, Gemini, Sagittarius, Virgo and Pisces, and all have an adaptability. They often appear selfless.

The third grouping is into positive and negative (otherwise known as masculine and feminine). In essence these are descriptive rather than definitive terms and equate in a general sense to being self-expressive or extrovert (positive) on the one hand and receptive or introvert on the other. This does not mean that if a woman has a masculine sign she is not to be considered feminine, and vice versa.

Taking into account the three groupings, the Zodiac signs are as follows:

Aries	fire, cardinal, masculine
Taurus	earth, fixed, feminine
Gemini	air, mutable, masculine
Cancer	water, cardinal, feminine
Leo	fire, fixed, masculine
Virgo	earth, mutable, feminine
Libra	air, cardinal, masculine
Scorpio	water, fixed, feminine
Sagittarius	fire, mutable, masculine
Capricorn	earth, cardinal, feminine
Aquarius	air, fixed, masculine
Pisces	water, mutable, feminine

When interpreting charts, another useful link between signs is *polarity*. This is the relationship between a sign and the opposite sign across the Zodiac. Thus, on a circular display of the twelve signs, Aries is opposite Libra, Cancer opposite Capricorn, Taurus opposite Scorpio, etc. The signs thus opposed do not, however, have opposite tendencies; rather, the polar signs complement each other.

Before turning to the concept of ruling planets, it will be helpful to consider a few other definitions and some lines and angles that are critical in the construction of a chart. The *ascendant* is defined as the degree of a sign (or the ecliptic) that is rising above the horizon at an individual's birth and marks the junction of the first sign. This is essentially the beginning for any astrological chart construction and interpretation, and after calculation is marked on the chart, working clockwise upwards from the horizon line, which runs east-west across the chart. The ascendant is very significant and can only be constructed if a birth time is known. The significance of the ascendant is that it indicates the beginning of the personality and how an individual faces the world—his or her true self. There are many other factors that may lessen the influence of the ascendant sign, but if some characteristic comes out of a chart that reinforces one linked to the ascendant, then it will be a very significant trait.

The *descendant* is the point opposite to the ascendant, at 180 degrees to it, and is always the cusp, or junction, of the seventh house. Although it may often be left out of charts, the descendant is meant to indicate the sort of partner, friends, etc, with whom one associates and feels comfortable.

The *midheaven* is often abbreviated to MC, from the Latin *medium coeli*. At the time when one particular sign of the Zodiac is appearing over the horizon (the ascendant) there will inevitably be another sign that is at its greatest height. This sign is then said to culminate at the upper meridian of the appropriate place—in brief, the midheaven is the intersection of the meridian with the ecliptic at birth. The significance of the midheaven is that it relates to the career of an individual and the way in which it is pursued. It can also provide a general indication of aims and intentions and the type of partner that may be sought. The point opposite to the midheaven is the *imum coeli* and is connected to the subject's origins, his or her early and late life, and parental/domestic circumstances. The *imum coeli*, or IC, is sometimes referred to as the nadir, but strictly speaking this is incorrect. The nadir is actually a point in the heavens that is directly opposite the zenith, which itself is a point in the heavens directly over any place.

Influence of the planets

Every sign of the Zodiac has what is called a *ruling planet*, which is the planet that rules the ascendant sign. From the list below, it can be seen that if someone has Pisces rising, the ruling planet will be Neptune. Each planet rules one sign, save for Venus and Mercury, which each rule two. Of course, before William Herschel discovered Uranus in 1781 there were only seven planets (including the Sun and Moon) and therefore three further planets ruled two signs; Saturn ruled Aquarius in addition to Capricorn, Jupiter ruled Pisces in addition to Sagittarius, and Mars ruled Scorpio in addition to Aries.

There are also a number of planets that are termed personal. The *personal planets* are the Sun and Moon (which are always personal), the planet that rules the ascendant sign (called the chart ruler). The Sun ruler is the planet that rules the Sun sign, and the planet that rules the sign occupied by the Moon is called the Moon ruler.

These different rulings were established a long time ago. There are additional features and weightings given to the rulings, known as *exaltation, detriment* and *fall*. Each planet is exalted when it is in a particular sign from which it works well and with which there is a notable similarity, resulting in more significance being attributed to it in an interpretation. The exaltations are also listed below:

Planet	Ruling in	Exalted in	Detrimental in	Fall
Sun	Leo	Aries	Aquarius	Libra
Moon	Cancer	Taurus	Capricorn	Scorpio
Mercury	Gemini	Virgo and Virgo	Sagittarius	Pisces
Venus	Taurus	Pisces and Libra	Aries	Virgo
Mars	Aries	Capricorn	Libra	Cancer
Jupiter	Sagittarius	Cancer	Gemini	Capricorn
Saturn	Capricorn	Libra	Cancer	Aries
Uranus	Aquarius	Scorpio	Leo	Taurus
Neptune	Pisces	Leo	Virgo	Aquarius
Pluto	Scorpio	Virgo	Taurus	Pisces

The ruling planets and relationships

Opposing the ruling sign of the Zodiac, each planet also has a sign of detriment. In this the planet is said to be debilitated. Finally, in this section comes the sign opposite to exaltation, which is called the fall sign. This is the sign opposite to the sign of exaltation and, is where the planet is thought to be weak. (*See* list on the previous page).

The Houses of the Chart

The astrological chart is divided into houses—in effect this is a way of subdividing the space around the Earth. There are numerous such systems, which have been devised over the years and which fall into three groups: the Equal House System; the Quadrant System; and a variation on these systems.

The *Equal House System* is one of the oldest and after a period of disuse is now back in favour. The ecliptic is divided into twelve equal parts, and the houses are marked by great circles that meet at the poles of the ecliptic and start by going through the degree of the ecliptic ascending over the horizon, and then through every point 30 degrees farther around.

The main *Quadrant Systems* are called after the people who developed them, for example, Campanus, Regromontanus and Placidus, and appeared in the thirteenth, fourteenth and fifteenth centuries respectively. The system of Placidus was used almost exclusively until the early 1950s because it was the only system with published reference tables. It was, however, the only system that did not utilize great circles as the boundaries of the houses.

The final system, a variation, includes the system of Porphyry, which has its origins in antiquity. This is based on the Quadrant System, producing four unequal divisions that are then equally divided into three.

The Equal House System is probably the simplest to use, and in it each house has a certain relevance or significance, affecting a particular aspect of life. The first six houses are concerned with a personal application while the last six apply more to one's dealings with other people and matters

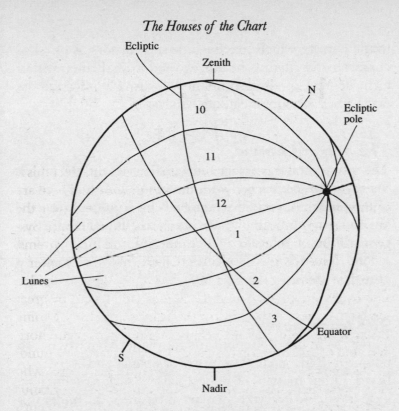

The Equal House System

outside the home and family. There follows an expanded though not comprehensive description of each house, stipulating the association of house with sign and planet and the resulting meanings. In this context, the planets stand for the provision of an impetus; the signs show how and where that impetus or motivation is to be used; and the houses indicate in which aspect of life the result will be seen.

The first house
This house is associated with Aries and the planet Mars, and because it includes the ascendant, or rising sign, is the most important house of the birth chart. This house refers

to the person, which may include such factors as physical characteristics, nature, health, ego and so on. Planets within eight degrees of the ascendant will strongly affect all aspects of the person, including behaviour.

The second house

The second house is associated with Taurus and the planet Venus, and is concerned with the possessions and feelings of the person. As such, this house reflects attitudes to money, and since money and love are intimately entwined, this aspect will be of relevance when interpreting a chart. The second house is also concerned with priorities and the growth of things.

The third house

This is the house of Gemini and the planet Mercury, which not surprisingly means a concern for siblings and also neighbours. Other matters of a local nature, such as schooling, local travel and everyday matters of business, fall under this house. Mental attitude, also falls into the third house, meaning that many important patterns of behaviour, can be considered here. Decisions such as where to live and personal environment are typical examples. All aspects of communication also fall within this house. For anyone who is lost as to what decision to take, a positive influence from the third house will help him or her.

The fourth house

The sign of Cancer and the Moon are associated with the fourth house. The key concerns of this house are the home itself, home circumstances and the family, and caring for someone or something. The mother, or a mother figure, is a particularly strong feature of this house. The concept of the home and the protective enclosing also has analogy with the womb and the grave—thus, the beginning and end of life are also concerns.

The fifth house

This house is very different from the fourth, and the association of Leo and the Sun makes it the house of pleasure and creativity. This includes all such aspects, whether they be related to art, authors, games, gambling, and other leisure pursuits. Moving into the more personal sphere, the fifth house also accounts for lovers and love affairs, probably on a superficial level rather than a lasting, deep relationship. The other personal manifestation of creativity, that of producing children, and parents' feelings about children and procreation, fall under the rule of this house.

The sixth house

The sixth house is the last that impinges upon the person and personal acts, behaviour and relationships. Its sign is Virgo and the planet is Mercury. This is a very functional house, referring as it does to work of a routine nature, health and similar matters. The work may be in the work place, hence it also relates to employers, or at home in the daily round of chores. The concern of health also includes diet, and this house will help to assess the need and timing for a change.

The seventh house

The last six houses refer to the wider influences of one's life and to outward application. Libra and the planet Venus are associated with the seventh house, and the fundamental concern is with relationships with others. This house concerns commitment in partnership and can reflect the likely type of partner sought. It can also relate to the establishment of a business or the employment of new people, from the viewpoint of personal interaction. Because this house encompasses dealings with others, it can also include hostility and conflict.

The eighth house

This house, the opposite of the second, is associated with Scorpio and Pluto, and refers to possessions gained through others, whether as gifts or legacies. In fact, all financial matters fall within this house. It is also the house of birth and death, or alternatively beginnings and endings. Deep relationships, including those of a sexual nature, are dealt with, as are matters of the occult and the afterlife.

The ninth house

The ninth house, the house of Sagittarius and Jupiter, is from the opposite of the third, which is concerned with neighbours and matters local. The ninth focuses upon travel to foreign countries and extensive study, and also has been called the house of dreams. Longer-distance communication and matters such as the law and literature are covered by the ninth house. Indeed, all factors that potentially may increase one's experience or awareness are appropriate.

The tenth house

The tenth house is the opposite of the fourth house and looks outward to life in general, being concerned with hopes and ambitions and making one's way in life. It used to be called the house of the carer and the father, when perspectives and opportunities were more limited than today. As such this is the province of the long-term carer and also denotes responsibility in the context of the delegation, both giving and receiving. This house is pertinent when career changes are considered, and is associated with Capricorn and Saturn.

The eleventh house

The eleventh house is associated with Aquarius and Uranus. It is the house of acquaintances, social contacts and friends (but not close friends), and as such may encompass societies, clubs and similar groupings. It also provides an indication of whether a person looks favourably upon charitable causes and whether any activities in this direction are genuine or for the self—the house of social conscience in effect. It was called the house of hopes and wishes.

The twelfth house

The twelfth house, associated with Pisces and Neptune, is linked with things that are hidden, self-sacrifice, psychic matters and also matters of an institutional nature. This last aspect may refer to hospitals or prisons, and as such may include the more serious illnesses. It can also shed light on problems of a psychological nature, reflected to some extent in its previous name—the house of sorrows.

The following section on Sun signs provides more information on personality, characteristics, associations and aspects of personal involvement and interaction.

The Sun Signs

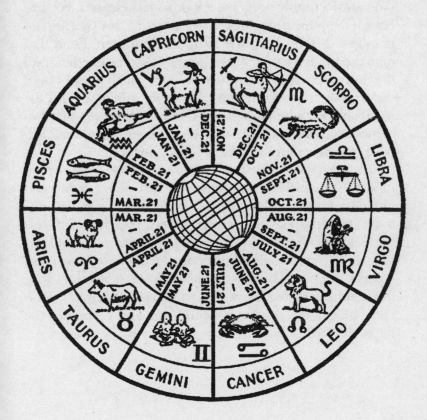

The cusps of the signs

One point should be carefully noted and borne in mind. The Sun enters each sign of the Zodiac on or about the 21st of each month, but it is still influenced to a certain extent by the attributes of the preceding sign, which do not fade away entirely until a week or so has elapsed. For this reason the pure and unmixed attributes of any sign are not manifested until about the 27th of the month. From that date the full force of the sign continues to be exerted until the Sun prepares to enter the next sign, which occurs about the 21st of the next month, and then, mingling with the influence of the new sign, gradually fades away and becomes extinguished in about a week, that is, about the 27th, when the new sign displays its full vigour.

This period—from about the 21st to the 27th of any month—in which the influences of two signs overlap and mingle, is known as the 'cusp' of the signs, and persons born at this time partake in a greater, or less, measure of the attributes of both signs. In estimating their character and fortune, both signs should be taken into account. For instance, a person who was born on September 25, a few days after the Sun has entered Libra, but with some of Virgo's influence still in force, is ruled by both Virgo and Libra, and the pages devoted to both of these signs should be consulted.

Aries

Dates

21 March to 20 April. The Sun enters the zodiacal sign Aries on approximately March 21 each year, remaining in this sign until about April 20. For the first seven days or so of its occupancy it is still influenced by the gradually declining power of the preceding sign, Pisces; so that persons born between March 21 and 27 are to some extent ruled by Pisces, as well as by Aries.

Origin and glyph

The ram's horns, which may be traced back to Egypt.

Ruling planet and groupings

Mars; masculine, cardinal and fire.

Typical traits

Most people born under the sign of Aries (the Ram) are full of energy. They often react like a battering ram, barging ahead with horns out and head tucked under, with little regard for either themselves or others.

Arians often give the impression of being very self-confident. But do not be fooled by appearances. They are really just as insecure as the rest of us. They are simply much better than most people at covering it up.

Arians are almost as vain as they are brave. They love to be popular and the centre of attention. And they spend a lot of time on their appearance.

Arians are no good at deceit or pretence. They are honest and direct people, but they tend not to think before they speak or act. So they can easily offend or hurt other people. Aries is known by astrologers as a fiery and positive sign, and is aptly symbolized by the ram, an animal of great courage and spirit. Aries is ruled by the planet Mars, and those born during this period are notable for their action, energy and initiative. In life's battles they play the part of guides and leaders; they glory in fighting and in surmounting difficulties, and their courage and self-confidence make them pioneers in all kinds of enterprises.

Arians have several noticeable characteristics, such as courage, seemingly boundless energy, enthusiasm, initiative and enterprise, and a desire for adventure and travel. This means that when faced with a particular challenge, there is a tendency to rush in without heeding the consequences, and this can often cause problems. This impulsiveness is, of course, one of their less appealing traits, and it may also be accompanied by selfishness. This manifests itself in the need to accomplish set tasks and reach planned goals, although they tend to have the beneficial quality of being able to concentrate on the primary aim by removing anything that is unnecessary and of little importance. Competitiveness is never far from the surface for an Arian, no matter what aspect of life is involved.

Their aptitude for responsibility and command gains them an ascendancy over others, and they are never so happy or so well employed as when they are supervising or directing a difficult undertaking, and imparting some of their own boundless enthusiasm to their followers and employees. As an example, we will mention Sir John Franklin, the famous Arctic explorer, who was born on April 16, 1786—a man marked out by destiny to be a natural leader of others, and one whose guidance was followed without question to the remotest parts of the earth.

The ambition of persons ruled by Aries knows no bounds, nor does their ability to overcome obstacles. Therefore, provided their interest in their occupation is sustained, they are fated more than all other types to rise to the head of any affairs in which they may be actively concerned. They are, however, impatient and rather capricious, and are apt to lose interest in an undertaking that does not promise to engross all their activities. Moreover, they will not brook the slightest opposition or contradiction; having implicit faith in their own abilities and in the cause which they have es-poused —whether it be right or wrong—they will impose their will upon others and override their opinions, and even when proved to be in the wrong they will seldom admit the fact.

Prince Bismarck; (born April 1, 1815), the 'man of blood and iron,' was ruled by Aries, and his autocratic, domineer-ing and fearless character illustrates the truth of what has been stated.

The outstanding defects of Aries subjects are rashness and excessive self-confidence, which often bring about their ruin. Aries people are inclined to outstrip the bounds of discre-tion in every direction, and they seldom learn restraint from past disasters. By their excessive frankness and boldness of speech they frequently make themselves detested, and by their unwarranted optimism and temerity they bring mis-fortune upon themselves and others.

Though they are splendid organizers and have the ability to see far ahead, they seldom work according to fixed and well-laid plans; in fact, scheming and subtlety of any kind are foreign to them, and they prefer to be guided by their natural intuition and presence of mind rather than by rules and precedents or a matured course of action.

Aries subjects cannot be led or compelled; but they can easily be deceived or seduced. Having little guile or sub-tlety in their own make-up, they fail to recognize it in oth-ers. Thus they can be influenced by suggestions cunningly made, and are readily deceived by praise and flattery, often of the most gross and obvious kind. Then, inflated by con-ceit and arrogance, they can be made to view things in a distorted way, and may be impelled to a course of action which, of their accord, they would never have contemplated; whereas any open attempt to control or overrule them would be met with instant, and often violent, opposition. If an Aries subject is convinced that he or she has been deceived or made to appear a fool, his or her anger is terrible to behold and the deception is never forgotten, although at other times he or she is among the first to forgive injuries and slights.

The highest type of person born under Aries is a resolute idealist. He or she or she will fight to the bitter end in the cause that he or she holds dear, and will sacrifice everything for it, and opposition—even persecution—only makes the fire of his or her conviction burn the brighter.

Idealists of this type were William Booth, the founder of the Salvation Army, and Albert, king of the Belgians; both of them were born under the rule of Aries, and both suffered for convictions which they would not abandon.

Relationships and love

Subjects of Aries are not easy to get on with in married life, especially if their partner refuses to give way in everything, as he or she would be expected to do.

Moreover, they seem quite at a loss to understand the psychology of the other sex, and their want of tact often causes pain. But they will always rise in arms to defend their spouse and children from the attacks of other people, and they are assiduous in providing for their comfort. Aries folk often suffer acutely through their affections and feelings, though their intense pride impels them to appear unmoved. Women belonging to Aries often gain a distinct advantage, socially and financially, upon their marriage.

In personal relationships, Arians can be very passionate, and Aries men look for a strong partner. Arian women are equally demanding and often prefer a career to being at home, although the two can be combined. Providing there are no adverse influences elsewhere on a person's chart,

Arians are faithful but there are those who are continually moving on to new relationships and challenges.

As parents Arians are, not unexpectedly, energetic and in the main will encourage their children in a variety of activities. It is all too easy, however, for the ebullience of the parent to overshadow the wishes of the child, and that can easily result in discord.

If you have an Arian as a friend there is no chance of getting bored, because he or she will be on the go all the time. Arians love a lot of social life and know tons of people. But they are also rather naive. They find it hard to distinguish between real friends and those who just hang on to enjoy the nonstop party. Sometimes Arians have too high an opinion of other people and therefore suffer disappointments when they are let down or slandered by acquaintances.

Arians are very faithful to their friends and are willing to do a lot for them. But they get very disappointed and cross if their efforts are not appreciated.

It is usually great fun having an Arian as a partner. He or she will be enthusiastic and very romantic. But it may prove difficult to hold on to an Arian, as they do not like being tied down. And they get bored very quickly and always like something new.

Arians don't mind having several partners at the same time. On the other hand they get furious and very jealous if their partners have the same idea.

Deep down, the Arian is pretty insecure, so if you are in love with one, you must remember that he or she has a great need to be reminded frequently of your love.

The most harmonious partnerships in friendship and marriage for Aries people are formed with those born between July 21 and August 21 and between November 21 and December 21.

Occupations

To satisfy the Arian character, an occupation ought to be challenging, with goals to aim for and with the opportunity to lead. Boring, routine jobs would not satisfy, but if that were the outcome then other activities would have to compensate. Large organizations with some freedom and a defined career structure, such as teaching, the police or the civil service, would be appropriate.

Natives of Aries excel in any occupation in which they can organize, express themselves and give full rein to their abundant intellectual powers. Therefore, they do well as explorers and pioneers, soldiers, leaders of reform and temperance movements, directors and heads of business concerns, political leaders, surgeons, nurses, editors, scientists, inventors and innovators. If they are artistically gifted, they often achieve fame as writers, painters and musicians. Raphael, the great Italian painter, Swinburne, Wordsworth, and Hans Andersen were born under Aries, as also were Johann Sebastian Bach, René Descartes, and William Harvey who discovered the circulation of the blood. All these men were innovators in their various ways, men who refused to be fettered by rules or custom.

Children

Children of this sign tend to show the typical traits of liveliness and enthusiasm, but because there is always an underlying impatience, a child may soon lose interest and be looking for something new. Performance at school may be chequered because of this trait. However, should such a child lose his or her place or standing, his or her natural competitiveness and wish to lead usually reassert themselves, and lost ground is regained and held.

Arian children get into a lot of scrapes. They often walk around with cuts and bruises and covered in plasters. They seem to be in such a hurry all the time that they can't be bothered to watch out for anything, so they are always bumping into people and things.

Most people learn from their mistakes. For instance if a child tumbles head over heels down the stairs, it will take more care next time. Not so the Arian, who doesn't take the tumble very seriously, soon forgets the incident and does the same silly thing all over again.

When parents of Arian children buy Christmas presents, they must remember to find a really good hiding place. Because Arian children are extremely inquisitive and are bound to find the presents and unpack them.

Arians show signs of leadership from a very early age. They are dominating and want to decide everything. If you tell a two-year-old Arian child not to do something, he or she will either have a temper tantrum or just defy you and do just what he or she pleases anyway.

But before too long has passed, it will be as good as gold and have forgotten the whole thing.

Good advice

An obvious word of advice for the Arian is to try to be a little more patient. And perhaps being a little more diplomatic would be a good idea too.

Fire and earth compatibility

The fire signs are not very compatible with the earth signs. Every time an Arian becomes enthusiastic about something, the Taureans and Capricorns will be real party-poopers and try to bring the Arian down to earth again. And if there is one thing an Arian cannot abide, it is being contradicted and told that one's ideas are a load of rubbish.

Of the three earth signs, Arians get on best with Virgo and worst with Capricorn.

Fire and air compatibility

Whereas earth can smother a fire, air is necessary for it to burn and flare up. So an Arian can get lots of encouragement for even the craziest of ideas if he or she sticks to a Gemini or an Aquarian. On the other hand they tend to lose contact with reality, so the ideas often come to nothing.

Of all the air signs, Arians get on worst with Librans.

Fire and water compatibility

Everyone knows that water puts out fire. So the combination of fire and water is not very good. The sensitive Piscean or Cancerian cannot understand the Arian person at all. And for his or her part, the Arian feels that water sign people are far too careful and considerate.

Of all the water signs, Arians get on best with Scorpions.

But of course we don't want you to drop all your friends who don't belong to the right sign! For even though you may be very different, it doesn't necessarily mean that you are going to quarrel.

On the contrary, you can grow to understand those who think differently to you. And perhaps they can teach you things you are not so good at.

Health

Aries rules the head, brain and face, and its subjects are liable to suffer from ailments and accidents affecting these parts, such as headaches, concussion, apoplexy, disorders of the eyes, nose and skin of the face, as well as cuts, burns, bruises and other head wounds. The stomach and kidneys may also give trouble at times. In other respects, the health is usually good, owing to the strong vital force imparted by Aries and its ruler, Mars.

To attract good vibrations

Those who would obtain the utmost from life should endeavour to attract harmonious astrological vibrations. The native of Aries should wear, and be surrounded with, bright colours, especially bright green, pink and yellow; however, all shades of red are good. White is also fortunate, but should not be worn entirely unrelieved by any other colour.

Wider aspects

In their other pursuits, Arians import their eager approach, which in certain circumstances can be positively damaging, for example, knocks and bruises in the early years.

Associations

Animals—ram, tiger, leopard.
Bird—magpie.
Colour—red.
Day—Tuesday.
Flowers—gorse, wild rose, thistle, honeysuckle.
Food—traditional rather than exotic.
Gemstones—the most fortunate stones for those born in this period are the ruby, bloodstone and diamond. One of these gems should always be worn about the person to ensure good luck.
Metal—iron.
Numbers—seven for Aries; nine for Mars.
Trees—holly, thorn, chestnut.

Famous Arians

Jeffrey Archer	Author
Warren Beatty	Actor
Samuel Beckett	Playwright
Maria Callas	Soprano

Giovanni Casanova	World's best known lover
Charles Chaplin	Comedian
Paul Daniels	Magician
Vincent van Gogh	Painter
Franz Joseph Haydn	Composer
Gary Kasparov	Chess player
Steve McQueen	Actor
Eddy Murphy	Comedian
James Parkinson	Physician
Diana Ross	Singer

Taurus

Dates

21 April to 21 May. The Sun enters the zodiacal sign Taurus about April 21 every year, and remains in this sign until about May 21. For the first seven days or so of this period (until about April 27) the gradually lessening power of Aries continues to exert its influence, and all persons born between April 21 and 27 fall under the rule of Aries as well as under that of Taurus.

Origin and glyph

The bull's head, which has links with early civilizations in Egypt.

Ruling planet and groupings

Venus; feminine, fixed and earth.

Typical traits

Taureans rely upon stability and security, both in an emotional and financial context, but granted this they can be extremely reliable, patient and tenacious. They tend to be persistent, methodical and see things through to the end, and this can be reflected in their steady progress through life, including their career. Their lack of flexibility can often lead to resistance to change, even when it is for the better. However, when facing the challenge, they usually cope better than most. Taureans are practical people who dislike waste, and they tend to have high standards.

Even though a Taurean may look calm and collected and ready to cope with any disaster, he or she can get as angry or upset as anyone. It takes quite a lot of doing, but once a Taurean is enraged it is definitely no fun being at the receiving end.

Taureans are very homely people. They love to have nice

things around them. They need to feel secure and love a warm and friendly atmosphere.

Taureans are usually very economical. This doesn't mean they are stingy, but they know how to handle their money and hate to have any debts. On the other hand they open both their hearts and wallets if one of their friends gets into trouble.

Taurus is an earthy sign and is symbolized by the bull, which represents nature and fertility. It is ruled by the beautiful and poetic planet Venus, and so it is not surprising that its subjects are usually distinguished by their love of beauty and harmony in every aspect of life, and by their intuition and sympathy with nature in all her moods. No matter how airy may be their flights of fancy, they never lose contact with the earth and terrestrial matters, and their imaginative and speculative powers are always tempered with sound common sense. This practical outlook is one of the leading traits of Taurus subjects; they are fond of work, and even those of the most refined type are not ashamed to work with their hands. They are particularly fond of gardening and any kind of labour connected with the earth and vegetation, but they are less successful in connection with animals.

Great pertinacity and fixity of purpose also characterizes the sons and daughters of Taurus. They will concentrate all their attention upon a single aim and refuse to be turned aside from their goal. They are usually of a happy and mild disposition and, though acutely sensitive of slights and rebuffs, are slow to anger. When thoroughly roused, however, the whole aspect of Taureans is completely altered, and they give way to furious and ungovernable wrath. Their unyielding determination does not desert them in anger, for they seldom forget an injury, and will fight their enemies unflinchingly to the bitter end. But they will have no part in trickery, deception and underhand dealings, which are quite foreign to their nature, so that all their battles are carried on in the open. As soon as an enemy shows signs of collapse, the Taurean is instantly sorry for him or her, and in this way frequently makes a fool of himself.

The receptive power of the Taurean mind is enormous; and natives of this sign are more powerfully affected by their associates and environment than are, perhaps, any other type of people. With their natural love of all that is harmonious and beautiful, they are deeply revolted by ugliness, squalor and strife and by coarse companions; and uncongenial surroundings of this kind reduce them to the lowest pitch of misery. On the other hand, they respond instantly to refined and sympathetic surroundings, when they give of their best. They make good and cheerful hosts, and are very successful socially—which is rather surprising, since their nature is usually retiring. Taureans have also a pronounced faculty for imposing their will upon others, which is probably another aspect of their strong intuitive powers.

Robespierre, whose birthday fell within the Taurus period, possessed this power of dominating his associates. It is seen in other types as well, especially in men of unusual intellect who have helped to mould the mind both of their contemporaries and their successors. Foremost among such is Shakespeare (born April 23, 1564), while others of this type include Joseph Addison, Alexander Pope, Machiavelli; Froude, William H. Prescott, Gibbon and Hume, the historians; Thomas Huxley and Edward Jenner, each of whom brought about a revolution in science; Herbert Spencer, the philosopher; and Robert Owen, the social reformer.

Natives of Taurus rarely have difficulty in attracting followers, either in business or for any kind of movement or project, but they should guard against being swayed by other people's advice instead of by their own good sense and intuition. They are often called upon to bear great responsibilities, which they do willingly and well, although not without becoming unduly worried.

Relationships and love

Subjects of Taurus have an intense love nature, which refuses to be satisfied with anything less than the entire affection of their marriage partner and friends. Being guided almost entirely by impulse, they frequently make disastrous mistakes in choosing a husband or wife. They demand perfection in their mate and are critical and exacting, as well as inclined to be unreasonably and violently jealous, but there is no malice behind their outbursts, which are only the natural result of the interplay between their strong physical nature and their acutely sensitive feelings. This makes them ardent and fascinating lovers, who know how to play at ill upon the emotions of their beloved as upon an instrument.

A good partnership is important to Taureans, and this means a happy harmonious partnership. Their need to put down roots can render them very good at making a home, as does the practical side of their character. They usually make good husbands and wives, and parents, but they may make the mistake of getting stuck in a rut. One of the faults of Taureans is jealousy and possessiveness, which can often be applied to a partner.

Having established a good home, Taureans will probably consider children to be very important, and the parents will strive to make their children happy. Babies and toddlers can be slow to reach the obvious milestones such as walking, but in later childhood things need to be learnt only once. Discipline is important because Taureans are essentially traditional and look for rules and guidance.

Subjects of Taurus will find that their most harmonious affinities and friendships are formed with those born between August 21 and September 21 and between December 21 and January 21.

Children

Taureans cannot stand being rushed or being forced to do something they don't want to. They can drive their parents mad in the mornings when everyone else is frantically getting ready to go to school or work. A Taurean child just won't hurry up. And if someone tries to force it, then there are tears and uproar all round.

And there is no point in trying to push them into the limelight. Parents who try to impress relations with their offspring's wonderful singing are in for a shock when their good little Taurus child suddenly becomes quite obstinate and refuses to do anything but wail furiously.

Even though Taurus children may seem to be lazy because they always take their time, most of them do well at school. They like to have everything in order, and their thoroughness stands them in good stead.

You will not find Taurus children causing trouble in the classroom. On the contrary, most teachers regard them as a bonus to the class, since they are good at concentrating on a subject and nearly always do their homework.

Taurus children like to draw and paint and they are quite likely to have artistic talents. Many Taureans are musical, and some of the most famous writers were born in the sign of Taurus.

Good advice

Taureans are not very good at handling their emotions and can be lazy. They will put up with a lot just to avoid an argument. But when pushed too far they become really incensed. So they would do well to solve their conflicts straight away, even though that may present some awkward moments.

Earth and water compatibility

The earth is only productive if there is enough water. Similarly, the down-to-earth Taureans and the more emotional water sign people such as the Cancerians and Pisceans can enjoy fruitful relations. Both groups enjoy nature and seeing things grow and prosper.

Scorpions are the only water sign people that Taureans do not get on so well with.

Earth and air compatibility

These two signs are not very compatible. The practical, careful and down-to-earth Taureans find it hard to swallow the fanciful ideas that the Libran or the Aquarian dream up. Their common-sense attitude swiftly dismisses these ideas.

For their part, air sign people often find Taureans very boring. And they get frustrated by the time it takes for a Taurean to make up his or her mind.

They may be able to work together, when the combination of Taurean thoroughness and the lively imagination of air sign people strikes a balance.

Taureans get on best with Librans and worst with Aquarians.

Earth and fire compatibility

Earth and fire signs are not very compatible either. Fire sign people tend to get extremely enthusiastic about things, and cannot bear to come up against a killjoy, who keeps trying to bring them back down to earth.

For their part, Taureans cannot bear to be with people who keep wanting to change things all the time, and who also try to rush them because they think things are moving too slowly.

But of course we don't want you to drop all your friends who don't belong to the right sign. For even though you may be very different, it doesn't necessarily mean that you are going to quarrel.

On the contrary, you can grow to understand those who think differently to you. And perhaps they can help you with things you are not so good at.

Occupations

Although Taureans do not like taking risks, they are ambitious. However, they are more likely to stay with a job than to chop and change, and will quite possibly remain in uninteresting employment because the income is well nigh guaranteed. Sure handling of money and financial affairs comes easily to Taureans, and many find careers in the financial sector.

Subjects of this earthy sign are suited to any occupation in which their imagination can have full scope. Being naturally musical and artistic, they make good composers, singers and musicians, as well as poets, novelists and painters. Apart from Shakespeare and others already mentioned, Robert Browning, Dante Gabriel Rossetti, Anthony Trollope, Sir James Barrie, Alphonse Daudet, J.M.W. Turner, J. L. Gérôme, Albrecht Dürer, Joseph Haydn and Sir Arthur Sullivan were all born under the rule of Taurus.

The lower types make good gardeners and agriculturists, builders and decorators, and are successful in almost any occupation that is practical and creative. Taurus subjects also excel in ministering to the wants of others and making them comfortable, and hence they make splendid physicians, nurses, matrons, housekeepers and cooks.

An outstanding example is Florence Nightingale, 'the Lady with the Lamp,' who was born on May 12, 1820. Taureans are also congenially employed as house and estate agents, florists, soldiers and government officials.

Health

The typical subject of Taurus is, like his or her prototype the bull, endowed with a vigorous constitution and splendid health. If there is a weak point, it is usually the throat or neck, and attacks of sore throat, tonsillitis and catarrh are likely. But the commonest complaints afflicting Taurus people are probably those arising from excess and indiscretions of diet. Music has a profound effect upon them, and when ill, tired or run down they are more quickly restored to health by good music and refined surroundings than by any other remedy.

To attract good vibrations

Taurus subjects can attune themselves to fortunate vibrations, which will make their life harmonious and successful, by surrounding themselves with all shades of blue and incorporating it in their clothes. Indigo, too, will be found restful and soothing, but red should be avoided, except, perhaps, the softest shades of rose. All colours should be subdued, for Taureans have little need of stimulants.

Wider aspects

Routine is vital, and change or uncertainty makes them uncomfortable. They enjoy leisure pursuits but must guard against becoming too lazy.

Associations

Animal—bull.
Bird—dove.
Colour—pale shades, especially blue, pink and green.
Day—Friday.
Flowers—rose, poppy, lily of the valley, violet, myrtle and foxglove.

Food—generally like their food.

Gemstones—sapphire, emerald, turquoise, lapis lazuli and moss agate.

Metal—copper.

Number—six for Taurus, and for Venus also.

Trees—almond, apple, walnut, sycamore, pear, ash.

Famous Taureans

Fred Astaire	Dancer, actor
Salvador Dali	Painter
Queen Elizabeth II	Monarch
Duke Ellington	Composer, pianist
Ella Fitzgerald	Jazz singer
Dame Margot Fonteyn	Ballerina
Shirley MacLaine	Actress
Karl Marx	Author, founder of Communism
Florence Nightingale	Hospital reformer
Robert Owen	Social reformer
Michael Palin	Comedian, actor
Iggy Pop	Singer
Sergei Prokofiev	Composer
Anthony Quinn	Actor
Robert Smith	Singer
Koo Stark	Model
Barbra Streisand	Actress, singer
William Shakespeare	Playwright, poet
Leonardo da Vinci	Painter

Gemini

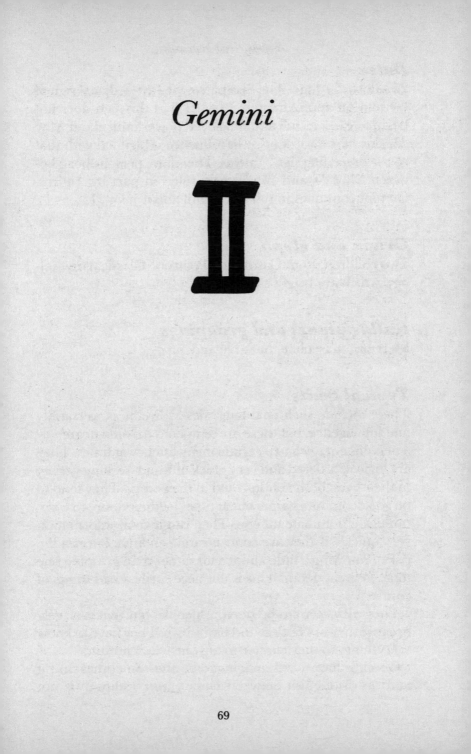

Dates

22 May to 21 June. The Sun passes into the zodiacal sign of Gemini on approximately May 21, but this sign does not begin to exert its full and unalloyed power until about May 27, since for a week or so its influence is blended with that of the preceding sign, Taurus. Therefore, persons born between May 21 and 27 are also ruled in part by Taurus. Gemini continues in full force until about June 21.

Origin and glyph

Two children, from Castor and Pollux of Classical mythology, which are bright stars.

Ruling planet and groupings

Mercury; masculine, mutable and air.

Typical traits

These include such characteristics as liveliness, versatility and intelligence, but these are tempered to some degree by a nervous energy and a certain inconsistency at times. They are logical, ordered and very quick of mind, seeking variety in their lives, both at home and in their work. They tend to be good communicators but at times let their desire to communicate dominate all else. They can take in information very quickly if they are concentrating enough, but run the risk of knowing a little about a lot rather than grasping one topic in great depth. This is not necessarily a bad thing, of course.

They may seem to be nervous people, but that is largely because they are restless and inquisitive. They have to know everything, so they chatter to anyone who's around.

Geminis have vivid imaginations, and sometimes find it hard to distinguish between fantasy and reality. It is not because they really want to lie: they just can't help embroidering on the truth.

A Gemini will often seem to be two different people at the same time. Madly happy one minute, and unbearably sad the next. And then five minutes later he or she will have forgotten what the problem was.

In ancient days Gemini was symbolized by twin children the Castor and Pollux of Roman mythology. Its astrological symbol consists of two columns united at the top and bottom, an apt illustration of the marked duality of mind and character displayed by those born under this sign. Gemini is known astrologically as an airy sign, and this again accords with the character of its subjects—subtle, intellectual, and versatile, but restless, undependable and diffuse.

The moral and intellectual make-up of a subject of Gemini is like a house divided against itself. This lack of unity is observable in all his or her actions, and often leads him or her into the most perplexing situations. Gemini is ruled by the restless planet Mercury, and a Gemini subject is truly 'mercurial' in everything, for he or she seems to be governed alternately by the attraction of two widely different poles. At one time he or she is full of ardour, energy and enthusiasm, with sparkling wit; but before long a sudden change occurs without any apparent cause, and he or she appears cold, lethargic and unresponsive. Gemini subjects are usually intelligent to a remarkable degree; their intellect penetrates rapidly to the root of any matter and strips it of difficulties, and thus they are extraordinarily apt at acquiring knowledge. But the interest soon wears off, and their attention wanders to something fresh and untried; and for this reason their knowledge, though covering a wide range of subjects, is, as mentioned before, seldom more than superficial.

In their relations with friends they are most undependable—at one moment affable and effusive, at another, so cold and unapproachable that the perplexed acquaintances are driven to conclude that unwittingly and unintentionally they must said something deeply offensive. But when next they meet the Gemini he or she is cordiality itself. However, when the mood suits them, the subjects of Gemini are remarkably good company, being exceptionally witty, merry, generous and—at least, to all appearances—sympathetic and considerate. Actually, however, this itself is only a passing whim or caprice, and they are only kind-hearted when it suits their mood of the moment.

Their nature being what it is, they crave change of scene and activity more than anything, and so are driven on by an insatiable thirst for travel and novelty. They are happy and successful travellers, being able to adapt themselves to any kind of circumstances and environment, though not for long will they make their home in one place, if they can avoid it. The famous African explorer, Sir H. M. Stanley, who was ruled by Gemini, is an outstanding example of this genius for travel.

Gemini people have very fair and unbiased critical faculties. They are able to look dispassionately at both sides of a question, and put themselves in the place of the other person. Their intentions are generally disinterested and honest, but are frequently spoiled by their lack of dependability.

They are often brilliantly clever, ingenious and inventive, and, given some fixity of purpose, there is no intellectual height to which they cannot climb, no depth of thought which they cannot sound. Among the striking instances of this superior Gemini type are Blaise Pascal, the great mathematician and philosopher, George Stephenson, of locomotive fame, Adam Smith, the economist, and William Pitt, who took the helm of State at the early age of twenty-four.

Gemini subjects are usually refined, possessing artistic tastes of a high order, and are gifted with wonderful tact.

Their keen penetration extends to their fellow beings, and they are excellent judges of character and ability. Since they readily divine the character and intentions of an opponent, and as a result are able to use his or her own weapons against him or her, they nearly always triumph in an argument or a battle of wits.

Most Geminis find it difficult to be punctual, since they are always being distracted by new things which they want to investigate. So if you make a date with a Gemini, you should be prepared to wait quite a while before he or she turns up (if indeed they do actually turn up).

Geminis have a great sense of humour, and if you have a good story to tell, you can be sure of a rapt audience. But if you start a long explanation with lots of small details they are bound to interrupt you or become bored: they probably worked out the punch line ages ago and can't be bothered to listen to all your waffle.

Their inventiveness and love of change causes them forever to be devising ingenious schemes or launching money-making projects, but these are often abandoned before they have a chance of coming to fruition. The lower types make clever crooks and sharpers, who usually succeed in evading detection.

Relationships and love

The Geminian curiosity and versatility render relationships a little more prone than most to disruption or diversion. However, partnerships can last, particularly if the husband/wife finds an interesting companion with whom he or she can interact intellectually. Gemini women often marry men who can deal with domestic chores, as such women have no love of housework.

As parents, they can be lively and creative but sometimes over-critical. It is not uncommon for Geminians to make poor parents because they can be too impatient, too heavily involved in their own careers and over-competitive, seeking reflected glory in their children's achievements.

Geminis seldom make do with just one friend. They prefer a whole crowd, and they like friends with lots of different interests.

Because Geminis are so restless, they can sometimes hurt their friends' feelings. Just when you think you are having a nice chat together, a Gemini will get up and disappear. And a moment later you will see him or her in deep conversation with somebody else at the other end of the room. He or she didn't mean to hurt you, but someone happened to turn up who was more interesting than you at the time.

Geminis don't like to talk about their feelings. You could say they are ruled by their minds more than their hearts, and so unless you are really good friends, it can be difficult to get to know a Gemini properly.

You must be prepared to share your Gemini with hundreds of other people.

The uncertainty of the Gemini temperament does not favour lasting friendship, and is the cause of much friction in married life. Moreover, those ruled by this sign are given to fickleness in their affections; they may lead a double life or commit bigamy. They are little swayed by passion, and the only way to retain their fidelity is constantly to meet their varying moods in a fresh and unexpected manner. All forms of monotony are fatal to success when dealing with Gemini people.

It can be something of a trial to have a relationship with a Gemini, because it often seems like having two sweethearts at the same time. Two twins, but definitely not identical. On the contrary, they are very different.

One day your Gemini can be so tender, that you are quite sure of his or her love. Then the next time you are together, your Gemini is cross and grumpy and finds fault with everything you do. Your clothes are horrid and your opinions are stupid, everything is wrong. Then shortly afterwards all is forgiven and forgotten again.

The Geminis' restless nature also means that they seldom stick to one partner for very long. They love to flirt around, although never very seriously. As they find it difficult to reveal their feelings, they will tend to back off if you try to get too close to them or to gain their full confidence. If you still persist then you run the risk of losing your Gemini.

Those who can live with them most harmoniously are born between January 21 and February 21 and between September 21 and October 21.

Children

Gemini children are likely to talk and walk relatively early, and it will be necessary to keep them well occupied. They have a knack of being in two places at the same time. Well, it seems that way anyway, especially to the poor parents who have to cope with a little Gemini.

It is often advisable to encourage them to finish anything they have started, to ensure numerous tasks are not left in various stages of completion. Because Geminians can also be quite cunning, and although they may be very able at school, they can often put their own thoughts before hard facts.

If a Gemini child starts getting bored in class, he or she will get out a comic and read it in secret under the desk. And because Geminis are adept at doing more than one thing at a time, they hardly ever get caught by the teacher.

Good advice

If you want to give Geminis some advice, tell them to slow down every now and then. But don't expect Geminis to crawl along like snails. They might also be advised to a spend a little more time with one pursuit, person or place before they go rushing off in search of something better.

Air and earth compatibility

People born under an air sign are seldom very happy together with an earth sign. They feel that the more contemplative Taurus or Virgo is too slow off the mark when the action starts.

On the other hand Gemini people do need to come down to earth occasionally when they get a bit too frivolous, and it does the earth sign good to 'get some air under their wings' now and then.

Of all the earth signs, Geminis seem to get on best with those born under the sign of Capricorn.

Air and fire compatibility

A Gemini is usually attracted by any idea, however crazy it may be. Leos and Arians are full of crazy ideas, so Geminis get on well with the fire signs.

However, when an air sign and a fire sign embark on a major project together, they can easily loose contact with reality. Their plans can flare up and fizzle out to nothing.

Of all the fire signs, Geminis get on best with Leos and Arians.

Air and water compatibility

As it is impossible to breathe under water, Geminis can feel suffocated by water people.

On the other hand, they have much to learn from one another. Water sign people are often very sensitive, and dealing with emotions is not one of the Gemini's strongest points. So perhaps a water sign person can teach the Gemini how to handle his or her emotions better.

Of all the water signs, Geminis get on best with Scorpions.

But of course we don't want you to drop all your friends who don't belong to the 'right' sign. For even though you may be very different, it doesn't necessarily mean that you are going to come into conflict.

On the contrary, you can grow to understand those who think differently to you. And perhaps they can help you with things you are not so good at.

Occupations

Geminians are very good when dealing with money and can, therefore, be admirably suited to banking or accountancy. As might be expected, the ability to communicate and the lively personality mean they may also fit well into employment in some aspect of the media or advertising. The pitfalls inevitably are that attention to detail may be lacking and that there must be variety. Conversely, they handle pressure well and are good at handling several tasks at once.

Those born under Gemini are most profitably engaged in work calling for mental gifts above the ordinary, as well as tact, subtlety, good judgment, and quickness of wit. They make excellent writers, journalists, teachers, secretaries, lawyers, barristers, magistrates, and diplomats, and are often successful as clerks, financiers, stockbrokers, and surveyors. They are usually very happy in any occupation involving travelling and constant change of scene and interest. People of the Gemini type often display literary ability of a high order, among the many outstanding examples being Lord Lytton, Emerson, Thomas Moore, Pushkin, Walt Whitman, Thomas Hardy, Sir Edwin Arnold and Charles Kingsley.

Gemini people are incredibly inquisitive and always on the hunt for new things to explore. On the other hand they find it hard to be thorough and steady at work, because they are always on the lookout for something new.

Geminis rarely make long-term plans. They live for the moment, and don't think about tomorrow. An ideal job for a Gemini is being a switchboard operator, or a secretary in a busy office where lots of different decisions have to be taken at once and where it would be handy to have as many arms as an octopus to get everything done.

The computer world is not a bad choice for a Gemini, both on the technical side as well as on the sales force.

Health

Gemini rules the shoulders, arms, hands and lungs, and its subjects may suffer from disorders and accidents to these parts. But their most common ailments are those affecting the nervous system (governed by Mercury, the ruler of Gemini). They are liable to nervous debility, nervous exhaustion, neuritis, mental strain and intense irritability, and their chief remedy lies in avoiding worry as much as possible.

To attract good vibrations

The colours most in harmony with Gemini are white, silver, yellow and light green. These should be worn on the person, and used freely in light furnishings and decorations.

Wider aspects:

Change and variety remain of paramount importance, whether in leisure pursuits or retirement. Individualism will dominate over group activities, which may become routine.

Associations

Animals—dog, squirrel.
Birds—parrot, linnet.
Colour—yellow, although most are liked.
Day—Wednesday.
Flowers—lavender, lily of the valley, snapdragon.
Food—salads and fruit, fish.

Gemstones—the most suitable stones for this period are agate, chrysoprase diamond and jade, but all gems that sparkle brilliantly are in harmony with Gemini.
Metal—quicksilver.
Number—five.
Trees—elder, filbert, any tree producing nuts.

Famous Geminis

Bjorn Borg	Tennis player
Joan Collins	Actress
Sir Arthur Conan Doyle	Novelist
Jason Donovan	Actor, singer
Bob Dylan	Singer
Gabriel Fahrenheit	Physicist
Peter the Great	Tsar of Russia
Stan Laurel	Comedian
Laurence Olivier	Actor
Alexander Pushkin	Poet, novelist
Brooke Shields	Actress
Queen Victoria	Monarch
Richard Wagner	Composer
John Wayne	Actor

Cancer

Dates

22 June to 22 July. The Sun enters the zodiacal sign Cancer about June 22 each year, remaining therein until July 22. However, the power of Cancer is not fully exerted until about June 27, and people born between June 22 and 27 are also controlled to some extent by the gradually declining influence of Gemini, which should be taken into account when their character and fortune are being estimated.

Origin and glyph

The glyph represents the breasts; Cancer probably came from ancient Babylon.

Ruling planet and groupings

Moon; feminine, cardinal and water.

Typical traits

The protective nature of the Cancerian is the overriding aspect of the character, but it is tempered by a stubborn and often moody streak. Although they tend to be of the worrying type, Cancerians have a remarkably good intuition, and their instinctive reactions and decisions can usually be relied upon. There is, however, a changeability about Cancerians that manifests itself in several ways. They can rapidly adapt to pick up information, habits, etc, from others. It also means that they can be touchy and, like the crab, may be hiding a soft, easily hurt person beneath a seemingly hard shell.

The symbol of Cancer is the crab, a creature whose habits typify the timid, hesitant yet tenacious disposition of those born under this sign. Cancer is known by astrologers as a watery sign, and it is ruled by the negative and watery Moon. Therefore, it is not surprising that this negative quality is the chief characteristic of those born under Cancer; it can be observed in all their actions and habits of life, making them shy, timid and retiring, constantly anxious over trifles, intensely sensitive, hesitant, romantic, dreamy, but unde-monstrative; their tenacity and powers of endurance are, however, little short of amazing. Having once committed themselves usually after much hesitation—to a definite course of action, they will pursue it resolutely until they have either achieved their goal or perished by the wayside. Of this type were Garibaldi, Mazzini, John Huss, and Calvin, all subjects of Cancer, and all notable for their fix-ity of purpose.

Few people are as sensitive as those born under Cancer. The least censure, criticism or lack of understanding is taken deeply to heart, but they respond with gratitude to appre-ciation and encouragement. However, they will not toler-ate interference in their affairs or in any project which they have undertaken, preferring to shoulder all the labour and responsibility rather than allow any meddling on the part of others. In uncongenial surroundings, or when tried by much opposition or lack of success, they become morbid and introspective; but they shrink to the last from opening their hearts to others, and jealously keep their worries and grief to themselves.

People of the Cancer type are often dominated by a fear of the future and old age. This may lead them to hoard money, and to become selfish and niggardly. However, they rarely want for money in actual fact, although their busi-ness affairs may pass through trying periods. They are very unsuccessful as gamblers, and their wealth—which is often excessive—is usually the fruit of persistent hard work, cou-pled with shrewdness, economy and foresight. Among the many sons of Cancer who have accumulated vast riches in this way may be mentioned John D. Rockefeller, Cecil Rhodes and John Jacob Astor.

Cancer subjects have most retentive memories, and this gift is often useful to them in their work, whatever it may be. They have also a great respect for convention, and are deeply interested in everything that is old, sacred or historical. At the same time, the freshness of unspoilt nature appeals to them strongly, and they are never so happy as when wandering in the woods and fields, especially in the neighbourhood of water.

Lower types of the Cancer subject are usually found to be indolent, greedy, mean, intensely selfish, suspicious, morbidly sensitive, and keenly resentful of imaginary injuries and slights. The higher types, however, who are hard-working, peace-loving and devoted to their families, provide one of the most valuable elements in the community.

Cancer is very close to the moon. And the moods of a Cancerian alternate according to the phases of the moon. Cancerians are very moody and so you never know whether they are going to be happy and cheerful or down in the dumps.

Cancerians are very sensitive to any kind of criticism. And since they also have incredible memories, one has to be wary of offending them. For they will remember an offensive remark for years to come.

Cancerians love secrets but don't expect them to tell you theirs. They definitely don't like discussing their private lives, although they love to hear all about yours.

Relationships and love

Affection runs very deep in Cancer folk, though they seldom wear their heart on their sleeve, so that their lack of demonstrativeness is often taken for lack of sentiment. They are happiest when in the heart of their family, to whom they are intensely devoted, but if, as is frequently the case, they consider that they are not properly understood by those dear to them, they become miserable and dejected, and retire within themselves. Their love affairs and domestic life are often full of worries and difficulties, which, however, are usually overcome by their great pertinacity and patience.

If you look at a picture of a crayfish, it looks as though it is about to give you a tremendous hug. Its 'arms' are spread wide open, waiting for you to fall into them.

But it also has very strong claws and keeps a powerful grip on you once it has latched on.

And that is what it is like to have a Cancerian partner. Cancerians take love very seriously, and because they are so fond of their mothers, they look for someone they can attach themselves to with the same degree of intensity. Some people may find them too possessive and stifling.

On the other hand, if you have a Cancerian friend, you can be sure of their loyalty: they will not run off with someone else at the drop of a hat.

If you examine a crayfish closely, you will discover that it has a hard outer shell which protects a very soft animal underneath. Without this shell it would be easy prey for its enemies.

People born under the sign of Cancer are also like this. They are very soft and sensitive and easy to hurt.

The caring nature of Cancerians makes them excellent at building a home and good at forming long-lasting partnerships. In general Cancerians like to look back in preference to forwards and commonly stay in the same house for a long period of time. A slightly negative aspect is that their protective nature can become excessive and turn into clinging, and they may be touchy and occasionally snap for no apparent reason.

The sensitive almost retiring aspect of the character can be seen quite early in life, and this may continue to the point that they become very shy at school; they may hide behind a shell. It is commonly the case that Cancerians will eye new social contacts somewhat warily, keeping them at arm's length. However, when they get to know each other better, firm friendships can develop.

Cancerians usually like their extended family within a reasonably short distance and are keen to help anyone who may need their support.

The Cancerian is a domestic animal, and does not have many friends outside the family. And because Cancerians are so touchy, they sometimes have difficulty in hanging on to their friends, who have to handle them with kid gloves.

You will not find Cancerian people quarrelling with their friends one minute and being best buddies the next. Or fighting with a friend on the way home from school and playing with him or her the same evening. They are fairly steadfast.

A Cancerian friend is a great help if you are unhappy. They are good listeners. And because they are so sensitive, they immediately sense what is the matter. In fact they may have guessed it even before you start to tell them.

Those born during the Cancer period will find their closest and most enduring friendships with people born between February 21 and March 21 and between October 21 and November 21.

Children

Cancerian children are good at signalling how sensitive they are. Their parents are particularly receptive and therefore constantly spoil their children and tell them how clever they are. So many Cancerian children get quite a shock when they emerge into the big wide world and do not meet the same level of consideration, and so they often spend the rest of their lives yearning for the lost security of their childhood and in particular for their mothers.

Try watching a crayfish chasing its prey, for example your big toe. It will not charge at the toe and grab it with its large claw. No, it will veer to the left, and then to the right, and maybe even recoil a bit, but all the while drawing closer and closer, and then suddenly snapping at it.

Children born under the sign of Cancer behave in a similar way when trying to reach some goal they have set themselves. If they want more pocket money or a new bike they will not demand it outright. Instead they will circle round the subject, maybe sidetrack onto something else, and finally get their way.

One of the school subjects which Cancerians are good at is history. They are very good at putting themselves into other people's shoes and if they read about a historical event, they almost feel as though they had been there themselves. So it's no wonder that they are able to remember it better than the others in the class.

After school a Cancerian will scour the area for odd jobs, offering to do anything from lawn-mowing in the summer to shovelling snow in the winter.

Good advice

We have already pointed out the extreme sensitivity of Cancerians. But they really need to learn that not all the unpleasant things said are meant as an attack. They could equally well be meant as good advice.

They also need to think about what they say themselves, because they are not nearly always so sensitive when it comes to other people's feelings.

Water and air compatibility

The air signs, Gemini, Libra and Aquarius, can learn from the water signs, and vice versa. For instance, Cancerians find it hard to grasp that other people are not made or think the same way as themselves. The air signs are better at this. In return, water sign people can teach the air signs to handle their emotions better.

Water and air are quite compatible. But just as water can suffocate air, for you cannot breathe under water, a Cancerian may have an over-possessive and stifling effect on an air sign.

On the other hand, air can churn water into high seas and a surging storm. And this happens when a Gemini or Libra makes no allowances for the more sensitive Cancer. Then the Cancerian mood is also likely to become tempestuous.

Of all the air Signs, Cancerians usually find their best friends are Aquarians.

Water and earth compatibility

Water is essential for all growth on earth. People born under an earth sign usually get on well with Cancerians. One lot are down-to-earth and sensible, the other more emotional. So if they do not try to dominate each other, but respect each other's idiosyncrasies, they can derive much pleasure from each other's company.

A plant can wither and die from over-watering, and a relationship can also founder if a Cancerian gives free rein to his feelings without any consideration of the more down-to-earth Taurean, Virgo or Capricorn.

Taurus and Virgo are the earth signs that Cancer people usually get on best with.

Water and fire compatibility

These two signs are usually not very compatible. Cancer people just cannot cope with Arians or Leos who come charging in at top speed and want to carry out some half-baked plan straight away.

In return, fire sign people often get annoyed with Cancerians who they feel are too considerate of other people's opinions and concerned about not offending others.

But of course we don't want you to drop all your friends

who don't belong to the right sign. For even though you may be very different, it doesn't necessarily mean that you are going to come into conflict.

On the contrary, you can grow to understand those who think differently to you. And perhaps they can teach you some things you are not so good at.

Occupations

Those who are ruled by Cancer are generally successful in occupations of a public nature, or those in which they can serve large numbers of people. On this account, they make good government officials, politicians, caterers and hotel proprietors. They often instinctively follow occupations connected with liquids, such as those of publican, wine merchant, barmaid, laundry proprietor and hydraulic engineer.

Cancerians can turn their hand to most things, and their careful, intuitive approach can make them successful. They tend to work well with people and often adopt the role of mediator, where diplomacy is required. The caring professions (for example, medicine) are obviously well matched to the Cancer character, but teaching may also be suitable. Although business may prosper under a Cancerian, there is often a tendency, even a fear, to change, which may show itself as inflexibility.

They are happy when on the sea, and make good sailors and naval officers. Many famous sailors have been born under this sign, including Paul Jones and Admiral Farragut. Success in finance and 'big business' often rewards the subjects of Cancer, so long as their activities are free from gambling and speculation. The literary and musical professions, especially if these bring them before the public, are also well suited to their romantic and imaginative temperament.

Health

Cancer governs the chest, the stomach and the higher organs of digestion. The most common accidents to which Cancer subjects are liable are chest injuries and broken ribs, while their most frequent ailments are bronchitis, pulmonary tuberculosis, pneumonia, pleurisy, dropsy, rheumatism and all diseases of the stomach. They should always try to exercise prudence and restraint in regard to what they eat, for they are naturally inclined to indulge over-freely in the pleasures of the table, with consequent indigestion and biliousness. Overindulgence in alcohol should in particular be guarded against, for Cancer subjects are liable to develop into drunkards. Finally, they should do all in their power to resist worry, their most potent enemy.

To attract good vibrations

Emerald green and glistening white are the colours most in harmony with this sign, and people of the Cancer type should always make a point of using these colours lavishly in their dress and in the decoration of their home.

Wider aspects

Cancerians are extremely sensitive, and while outwardly they appear charming and friendly, they can be temperamental and subject to wide mood swings. In general they love change, and while travel appeals, home has the greatest attraction.

Associations

Animals—otter, seal.
Birds—seagull, owl.
Colour—silver and pastel shades;
Day—Monday.
Flowers—poppy, lily, waterlily, white flowers, especially the rose.
Food—dairy foods and fish.

Gemstone—the best stones for this sign are emeralds and moonstones, though cat's-eyes, pearls and crystal are also in harmony.
Metal—silver.
Numbers—two for cancer; seven for the moon;
Trees—willow, sycamore.

Famous Cancerians

Pierre Cardin	Fashion designer
Marc Chagall	Painter
Dalai Lama	Spiritual leader
Princess Diana	Princess of Wales
Harrison Ford	Actor
Gina Lollobrigida	Actress
Gustav Mahler	Composer
George Orwell	Author
Sylvester Stallone	Actor
Ringo Starr	Drummer
Meryl Streep	Actress
Mike Tyson	Boxer

Leo

Dates

23 July to 23 August. The Sun enters the zodiacal sign of Leo on approximately July 23 each year, and remains therein until about August 21. But the full influence of this sign does not begin to exert itself until about July 27, being mingled until then with the gradually decreasing force of the preceding sign, Cancer. Therefore, people born on the cusp—between July 23 and 27—are also partly ruled by Cancer, and should study the influence of that sign as well.

Origin and glyph

It probably originated in ancient Egypt, from the constellation; the glyph resembles the lion's tail.

Ruling planet and groupings

Sun; masculine, fixed, fire.

Typical traits

Leonians tend to be generous, creative and yet proud individuals who nevertheless need to keep a tight rein on themselves to avoid becoming overbearing. The creative nature needs to find an outlet in whatever guise, and it is common for Leonians to become organizers, with confidence and energy, although beneath that they may be rather nervous. The possible risk is that Leonians may end up taking over and feel they always know best, so they must learn to listen to the views of other people. They can also display a temper, if only briefly, and are prone to panic if things go badly wrong. However, they generally regain control of the situation quickly. Their impatience and tendency to go over the top are countered by the abundance of their positive qualities.

Leo is a positive and fiery sign, ruled by the ardent, masculine and strongly magnetic Sun. It is symbolized by the lion, and the typical person born under this sign has much of the 'leonine' in his or her nature, including great courage, loyalty, energy, dignity, and a decided gift for leadership. Even his or her personal appearance is often leonine, for the purest and most representative types are distinguished by a tall, vigorous frame, broad back and shoulders, well-developed muscles, an erect carriage, a shock of yellow, golden or tawny hair, and a general appearance of pride and fearlessness.

Affection, sympathy and warmth of heart characterize people who are born under this sign. Their love embraces the whole of humanity, and their loyalty is such that they will defend their friends even to their own detriment, and will never desert one whose cause they have championed, unless disgusted by his or her treachery or deceit. Their nature is essentially so simple and noble that the least suggestion of guile or double-dealing is more hateful to them than anything, and is the only thing that can alienate their affection. They are utter strangers to fear, both physical and moral, and when roused are terrific fighters, but at the same time they will submit to a great deal of provocation before showing signs of anger. Then, no matter to what pitch of fury they may be wrought, they always fight fairly and according to the rules, and are invariably generous to a vanquished enemy.

Natives of Leo are direct and open in speech and the expression of opinions, but they are frequently tactless—for to them diplomacy savours of guile, which they detest. They are also inclined to be stern, severe and heavy in manner, even to those they love deeply, and are very quick-tempered when there is any suggestion of their honour or dignity being impugned.

Leos love to perform, and be the centre of attention all the time. If there is a boy trying to impress all the girls in the playground by balancing on the walls or doing something else to attract attention, then you can be pretty sure that he is a Leo.

Leos love flattery. And they lap up praise like a cat who has been given a bowl of cream. For they never doubt that people really mean it, and that they fully deserve it.

Leos are not the type to reflect on things. You can bet on it that the gentle boys, with whom you can sit and chat for hours, were definitely not born under the sign of Leo. On the other hand, Leos are often very generous and warm people.

Ask a Leo for a piece of advice, and you can be sure of his help. And don't be afraid to follow it. But do not try and return the favour, for good advice is something one dispenses to one's subjects, and as you know, a king has no superiors.

Leos do everything in the extreme. When Leos are on the go, there is a regular buzz of activity all around. But when they stop, they can be so incredibly lazy that they will not lift a finger and get everyone else to wait on them.

Their convictions usually become settled early in life, and are rarely changed or modified later; they are expressed dogmatically, even defiantly. The extreme Leo types are often very narrow-minded and bigoted.

Their ambition is great and their strength of will considerable, so that it is not surprising that they usually surmount all difficulties that lie between them and their goal. In obtaining their desires, they frequently appear ruthless; this is seldom the result of wanton cruelty, but springs from the belief that the few must be sacrificed for the ultimate good of the majority. Leo people are born to play the part of leaders, and they have the gift of inspiring rare devotion in those who believe in them. Striking instances of this type are the emperor Napoleon, Benito Mussolini, Cavour, and Simon Bolivar, all of whom were born under this sign.

In money matters Leo folk are usually favoured by fortune, and they may rise to the position of financial magnates; if they do, it will not be through trickery, but as a result of their own energy and natural gifts. They will wish to share their wealth with others, and will subscribe freely to charities, but at the same time will surround themselves with all the luxury and refinement that money can command; in the lower types, this will be manifested as vulgar ostentation. Indeed, a love of display characterizes all Leo subjects, and they have a marked predilection for all that flashes and glitters, especially gold, brass and bright metal objects, strong sunshine and brilliant colours.

The less highly developed Leo subjects may be boastful, vulgar and ostentatious, arrogant and tyrannical and possessed of a mania for popularity. They are usually absurdly sensitive on points of dignity, and may also be wasteful and recklessly extravagant.

Relationships and love

Being extremely affectionate themselves, Leo folk are ruled by affection, and they make the finest marriage partners, parents and friends—kind, loyal, and considerate. They can generally be ruled through their feelings (though not in any other way whatever), and they may be deceived or even led into doing wrong by playing on their sentiments. In love and marriage they make many errors and suffer deeply from them; they are prone to mistake pity and sympathy for love, and may realize their error when too late, but their natural generosity and forbearance often save their married life from shipwreck.

To their partners Leonians will be affectionate, but their strong will and urge to lead can make them rather domineering. However, they can be very sensitive, and criticism can cut deeply. As parents, Leonians understand and encourage their children and will do anything to ensure they are not unhappy. However, they are not over-compliant and often associate with traditional values when it comes to behaviour and education.

If you have fallen for a Leo man and you want to attract his attention, then you just have to flatter him and turn yourself into a willing audience.

In return you will get a real gentleman, who will protect you like a gallant knight and perform great deeds for your sake.

But you must realise that he is incredibly vain, and if you start offending him he will back off.

Of all the Sun signs, Leos are the first to start falling in love and to have sweethearts. And it is not all smooth sailing, because they are either up in the clouds or down in the dumps. And their mood can change a hundred times in the course of one day.

If you are a man who has fallen in love with a Leo woman, you will have to face a lot of competition. Leos are popular so if you have an inferiority complex you will have your work cut out to capture a Leo. Because a Leo woman knows just what she wants and won't settle for the first man who happens to come along.

And if you are the kind who likes to have your sweetheart sitting admiringly at your feet listening to you expanding on all your great ideas, then you would be well advised to find a woman who was not born under the sign of Leo.

Leos love to be in the centre of things and the constant focus of attention. So it is not always easy to have a Leo as a friend, since you must expect to stand on the sidelines. Many Leo girls choose to be friends with girls who are less pretty or less charming than themselves. So then there is little danger of the friend stealing any limelight from the vain Leo.

On the other hand you will never be bored with a Leo around. Sometimes one gets the impression that a Leo never really grows up.

But Leo people are also very caring especially towards the weaker members of society. They may complain about being lumbered with everything, but they don't really mean it. Actually they rather enjoy shouldering the whole burden themselves.

And they are also very generous. If you are short of cash you can more or less depend on your Leo friend coming up with a loan.

Those born under Leo have the closest ties of affection with people whose birthdays occur between March 21 and April 21 and between November 21 and December 21.

Children

Some children nearly always become the leaders of the social groups they move in. And they get very cross and touchy if they are not allowed to make all the decisions.

This description fits most Leos. They love to decide what's to be done and make the rules of the game. And actually they are quite good at it.

They don't only want to make all the decisions among their friends, but at home as well.

Boys born under the sign of Leo love to play dangerous games or war games. You won't find them borrowing their sister's dolls to play with.

Leo girls are sometimes dreadfully wild, but they are also quite vain. So they usually try to keep their clothes neat and tidy, rather than mucking them up by acting like tomboys.

Leo children tend to have an outgoing and bright personality, but they must not be allowed to be bossy towards other children, nor must their stubborn streak be allowed to develop. However, any criticism must be levelled in such a way as not to dent the rather fragile Leo self-confidence.

Leos often charm their way to gain higher marks than

they really deserve. Many Leos are really quite lazy when it comes to anything they have not chosen to do themselves.

Even though Leos seem so self-confident, they are also very vulnerable. The worst thing you can do to a Leo is to laugh at them. You are welcome to laugh with them, especially if the Leo is the one telling the joke. But since Leo people are very vain, they cannot bear to make fools of themselves.

Good advice

Even though Leo people may find it difficult, it would be a good idea if they occasionally took themselves less seriously.

Leos also tend to go the whole hog with things that interest them. It would be sometimes better both for them and those around them if they learned to take things more easily now and again.

Fire and earth compatibility

There is nothing more annoying than someone saying 'Stop making such a fuss' when you have taken out all the stops to convince them of your brilliant idea, or who just reacts to your grand plans with a derisive remark.

And as Leo people are the most vulnerable and vain of all the fire signs, they sometimes find it difficult to get on with earth signs, Taurus, Virgo and Capricorn. For the earth signs will try to bring the Leos back down to earth again, however enthusiastic they may be.

Of all the earth signs, Leos get on best with Capricorns.

Fire and air compatibility

Whereas earth sign people can suffocate a fire sign like Leo, the air signs fan their flames so they burn more strongly.

On the other hand, the two together tend to lose touch with reality. So if a Leo starts making great plans with a Gemini or a Libra, these often end up like castles in the air. Of the air signs Leos get on best with Librans.

Fire and water compatibility

People born under these signs find it hard to understand one another, so a Leo will rarely count a Cancerian or a Scorpio amongst his or her best friends.

Leos are always in too much of a hurry to make allowances for the water sign people, who they consider to be 'wet'. In return, water sign people think that Leos are too self-satisfied, egoistic and bombastic.

Of all the water signs, Leos get on best with Pisceans.

But of course we don't want you to drop all your mates and friends who don't belong to the 'right' sign. For even though you may be very different, it doesn't necessarily mean that you are going to quarrel.

On the contrary, you can grow to understand those who think differently to you. And perhaps they can help you with things you are not so good at.

Occupations

Whatever their occupation or position, Leo individuals will work hard, in part because they are happier when they have people working for them. For many, luxury or glamour will appeal, and if they can achieve this through their employment then so much the better. As such, they may turn to acting, sport or working in the jewellery trade. They will often go for highly paid jobs, which they equate with status, but, equally, they make good employers, expecting the best of their employees but generous in return. Leo produces rulers, soldiers, statesmen, church dignitaries, and governors, leaders and managers of every kind. Financiers, 'captains of industry', bankers, jewellers, and goldsmiths are also born under its rays. On the artistic side, the Leonine love of colour, action and display may produce talent for the stage, literature and painting. Famous Leo subjects so gifted being Mary Anderson, the actress, Shelley, Southey, Sir Walter Scott, De Quincey, George Bernard Shaw, Alexandre Dumas, Fenelon, John Dryden, Izaak Walton, and Jean Baptiste Corot, the painter. The Leo type is not happy when in a subordinate position, and cannot bear to be ruled or given orders; but he or she makes an able, though exacting, employer or manager. You will discover that many actors are born under the sign of Leo.

Health

The vitality of Leo folk is boundless; they have the ability to absorb the vivifying power of the sun to the fullest extent, and sunlight, coupled with fresh air, is their finest tonic and restorative, But they should be careful not to indulge overmuch in violent exercise, for there is danger of the heart being strained or weakened. The heart, spine, back and eyes are the parts of the body most liable to disease or injury. Heart trouble, palpitation, angina, spinal disease, lumbago, meningitis, and disorders of the eyes are among the commonest complaints of the Leo type; but they hate to give way to sickness, and will put up an heroic fight before being prostrated. It is fatal for Leo people to be idle, since they then become morose and gloomy; and when in good health they should be constantly occupied with some interesting employment.

To attract good vibrations

Those born in the Leo period should wear all shades of gold, yellow and orange, while light green and white are also suitable. Gold, and all bright, glittering objects, such as polished brass or copper ornaments, will be found lucky and should be kept about the house.

Wider aspects

The Leonian is better leading rather than following and excels where generalities rather than attention to detail are accepted.

Associations

Animal—lion.
Birds—cock, eagle.
Colour—gold and scarlet.
Day—Sunday.
Flowers—marigold, sunflower, cowslip, heliotrope.
Food—honey and cereals, most meats and rice.
Gemstones—ruby, all yellow stones, such as amber, chrysolite, tourmaline, topaz and sardonyx. These stones should be set in gold, since this is the metal of the sun, ruler of Leo.
Metal—gold.
Numbers—four for Leo; one for the sun.
Trees—citrus, walnut, olive, palm, laurel.

Famous Leos

Napoleon Bonaparte	Emperor
Emily Bronte	Novelist
Kate Bush	Singer, songwriter
Fidel Castro	Cuban leader
Christopher Dean	Ice skater
Paul Gallico	Author
Mata Hari	Spy
Alfred Hitchcock	Film director
Dustin Hoffman	Actor

Aldous Huxley	Novelist
Mick Jagger	Singer
Madonna	Singer, actress
Henry Moore	Sculptor
Robert de Niro	Actor
Peter O'Toole	Actor
Beatrix Potter	Author, illustrator
Yves Saint-Laurent	Fashion designer
George Bernard Shaw	Playwright
Terry Wogan	TV and radio Presenter

Virgo

Dates

24 August to 22 September. The Sun enters the zodiacal sign Virgo on approximately August 24 every year and leaves it on September 21. However, the influence of this sign does not begin to be fully exerted until about a week after the Sun's entry, being diluted by the force of the preceding sign, Leo. Therefore, persons born between August 24 and 27 are also partly ruled by Leo, and should consult the characteristics given by that sign as well.

Origin and glyph

The Egyptian goddess of grain (Nidaba) was probably the origin, and in old pictures the Virgin is shown bearing an ear of corn and holding a child; the glyph is the female genitalia.

Ruling planet and groupings

Mercury; feminine, mutable and earth.

Typical traits

Virgoans are traditionally shy and modest, hard-working and practical and yet, perhaps, rather dull. They have a well-developed tendency to criticize both themselves and others, and often allow this to go too far. If a positive tenor is applied to Virgoan traits, it results in someone who works hard, is sensible and intelligent, and very good at detailed tasks.

Being essentially a worker, Virgoans are not interested in taking the lead but more in completing a task to the best of their ability. There is a likelihood that Virgoans will be worriers, and they often worry about nothing at all, which can be misconstrued or counterproductive. However, their own positive qualities are the best tools to deal with such problems.

Virgo people are nearly always worried about something. They want everything to be in order, and they spend lots of time planning to ensure perfect results every time. They are incredibly conscientious and have such a tight check on things that for instance, they seldom have money problems.

It is not easy to criticise a Virgo, because they get terribly hurt. They find things hard enough as it is, because they feel that they never really live up to their own high standards.

Virgo people cannot get on with people who have sudden crazy whims. Don't expect your Virgo partner to get up in the middle of the night to make a lasagne just because you are hungry and can't sleep. They think that there is a time and place for everything.

The negative and earthy sign Virgo is associated with intellectual power, and subjects of Virgo are distinguished by the keenness of their wits and their remarkable discrimination. They are, perhaps, the most calm, level-headed and practical of all the twelve types, for they seldom allow a vestige of sentiment or affection to interfere with, or bias, their judgment or conduct. Indeed, it is probable that sentiment is very shallow in Virgo people, for even the superior types are notable for their selfishness. At the same time, these characteristics have a useful function to fulfil, for they act as a wholesome check upon the more impulsive and expansive types; and, by their critical judgment and cool reasoning ability, natives of Virgo help to avert many errors and catastrophes that would not be foreseen by more rash and emotional people until too late.

Virgo people are pliant and adaptable. They can readily vary their manner and behaviour to suit the company in which they find themselves; while their tactfulness may often amount to servility. But this is not the result of fear; it is usually part of a deliberate plan or scheme, carefully prepared beforehand, and with a definite end in view.

Virgo people are not usually acquisitive, but, should one born under this sign set his or her heart upon anything, he or she will stop at nothing to attain it, and, if he or she is of a lower type, he or she may display the most extraordinary cunning, hypocrisy and cold-blooded guile. Not even human life stands in the way of a person of the undeveloped Virgo type when once his or her mind has become fixed upon a definite aim. This type is also capable of displaying greater cruelty than any other; he or she can commit the most shocking injustices and barbarities in cold blood, and nothing will move him or her to pity when he or she is actuated by hatred or self-interest. Of this type were the emperor Caligula, Richelieu, Queen Elizabeth of England, and Abdul Hamid, ex-sultan of Turkey, the 'Great Assassin', all of whom were natives of Virgo.

Subjects of Virgo have the love of inquiry developed to the utmost; they are never satisfied to take anything on trust, but must always find out for themselves. Accordingly, under this sign many famous philosophers, mathematicians, and scientific investigators have been born, including Baron Cuvier, John Locke, Tommaso Campanella, Comte de Buffon, Baron von Humboldt, and the Marquis de Condorcet.

Generally Virgo people are modest and reserved; they shrink from publicity, and will not talk readily about their own affairs, preferring to criticize the actions of others and analyse their motives. They are lacking in enthusiasm, and show reluctance to fall in with the plans of others or to assist them in any way. They are entirely individual and quite lacking in camaraderie and the 'team spirit.' When pursuing their own objects, which they do in a steadfast, practical and matter-of-fact manner, they will listen noncommittally to the advice of others, but will seldom act upon it.

Their lack of sentiment makes them very slow to anger, but they are equally slow to forgive, and seldom compose a quarrel of their own accord. But they can swallow resentment and put their pride in their pocket when they consider it to be in their own interests to do so.

Virgo subjects are precise and methodical in all that they do, and have a great respect for law, order and precedent and for the achievements of the past. They are fond of harmony and elegance, and their taste is restrained and austere; but their imagination is decidedly limited, and is far exceeded by their reasoning powers. They are very fond of reading, and are able to remember very clearly a great deal of what they read and see.

The weaker varieties of this type are cunning, capricious and cruel in the extreme, cynical, unduly critical, caustic in their speech and perpetually finding fault. They are also snobbish, servile and excessively selfish.

Relationships and love

Virgo subjects are well suited to married life, being dutiful, faithful and proud of their family, though usually they are quite undemonstrative. The happiness of their union may depend upon their ability to control their proclivity for criticism and fault-finding.

Virgoans are very loyal in relationships and fond of their family, although this love may not manifest itself openly but rather in private. They may be self-effacing or even devalue themselves by feeling unworthy. A more common fault would be to over-criticize, but in the main they are caring, sound partners.

A great deal of time and attention will be paid to the home to keep it nice, but care should be exercised so that standards are not kept too high.

Virgos are very considerate people, and therefore make good friends, especially if you have problems and need some consoling. They are also very perceptive and so you would do well to consider any advice they give you. It is probably quite sensible.

However, it can sometimes be a bit tiresome having a Virgan friend because they are so critical. He or she will pick at your wildest plans until you have been convinced that they are no good and you might as well drop them.

A positive Virgan trait is their sense of humour—but you can save your dirty jokes for other people.

If you are a woman who has fallen in love with a Virgo, do not expect him to stand serenading you outside the house every night.

On the other hand you can be almost certain that he will never forget your birthday, or make you wait for him under the clock for half an hour, just because he had to watch the end of a football match on TV. If he says he is coming at a certain time, he'll be there.

Virgo people are very touchy, so if you manage to get invited to his house, and you are asked to stay for dinner, do remember all your best table manners. Virgos are sticklers for that sort of thing. And if his mother should also happen to be a Virgo, she will like you instantly and consider you to be the ideal partner for her son if you polish off your food so your plate looks as though the dog has licked it clean—just as long as you don't lick it yourself!

Men who are trying to impress a Virgo woman should not let themselves be led to mistake the Virgo sense of humour for an interest in farting and belching competitions! Any attempt in that direction will meet with instant rejection. And you will not fare much better if you try telling the latest dirty jokes.

A Virgo man is not likely to succumb to the allure of the topless girl on the beach. He is more likely to offer her his jumper, thinking that she may be freezing.

However, many Virgo people love to flirt. And they are good at it. But that does not mean that you are destined for a long-term partnership. In fact, there is evidence to prove that more Virgos remain single than any of the other sun signs.

But if you do manage to hook a Virgo, which can be very difficult because they are so critical, then you can count on a very faithful and stable partner for life.

Their best affinities for marriage and friendship occur with those born between April 21 and May 21 and between December 21 and January 21.

Children

Virgo children usually get on well with their parents. They don't mind doing the washing up, and they may even volunteer their services unasked. Virgos are also spared another one of the standard quarrels between parents and children. Many of you who are not Virgos will recognise the classic conflict when your parents keep complaining that you never clear up your room and that it looks like a pigsty. This doesn't happen when the children are Virgos.

Virgo children like to be kept occupied and at school and will be neat, tidy and helpful. Their natural shyness may make them seem aloof, but if they can build up their self-confidence this will help them to keep worry at bay.

Virgos are often the teacher's pet. They are never late, have always done their homework and have never forgotten their pens or calculators.

It is a good thing that Virgo people are so conscientious, because they can't handle being told off. Other pupils may be able to take the teacher's reprimands without batting an eyelid, but Virgo people feel quite crushed. And any scolding tends to influence their interest in, and enjoyment of school for a long time afterwards.

Good advice

Virgos can drive others round the bend with their obsession for cleaning and perfection in everything. They really ought to remember that there are more important things in life than whether every nook and cranny is clean. And they should also stop worrying so much. Some even get quite sick from worry.

Earth and water compatibility

People born under a water sign are very emotional and therefore often get on well with the more down-to-earth Virgo. For the earth to bear fruit, it needs to be watered, but too much water will drown the plants. The relationship will founder if one of the parties becomes too dominating. Of all the water signs, Virgos find it hardest to get on with Pisceans.

Earth and air compatibility

These two signs are not very compatible. The practical, careful and down-to-earth Virgos cannot take the fanciful ideas that Geminis, Librans or Aquarians come up with. Their need for a few common sense details will smartly topple all those vague notions.

In return, the air signs consider Virgos rather boring, and think that they take too pragmatic a view of life, never wanting to have any fun.

They may be able to work together on the odd occasion when the practical common sense of the Virgo combines well with the lively imagination of air sign people. But they do not make for good partners in love.

Of all the air signs, Virgo people get on best with Aquarians.

Earth and fire compatibility

The fire signs are bursting with energy and enterprise. On

the other hand Virgo people never undertake anything that has not been closely considered and planned down to the last detail.

These two signs usually find it hard to get on well. Virgo people do not understand how others can love new and exciting projects, and enjoy living at high speed. They prefer a routine and like any new project to be preceded by a thorough and detailed planning process.

But of course we don't want you to drop all your friends who don't belong to the right sign. For even though you may be very different, it doesn't necessarily mean that you are going to quarrel.

On the contrary, you can grow to understand those who think differently to you. And perhaps they can help you with things you are not so good at.

Occupations

The critical and analytical faculties with which natives of Virgo are endowed make them well fitted to enter the law or politics. Among well-known lawyers, politicians, and statesmen born under Virgo were Sir Edward Marshall-Hall, Lord Oxford and Asquith, Bonar Law, Sir Charles Dilke, Lord Burleigh, Sir Robert Walpole, Richelieu, Colbert, Lafayette, Louis Kossuth, President Taft and President Diaz.

Virgo also favours the occupations of literary pursuits, music, and dramatic critic, editor, doctor, policeman and detective. Mercury, the ruler of Virgo, governs clerical work; therefore the professions of secretary, accountant, schoolmaster, printer and stationer are also indicated. The accuracy and precision of Virgo produce good chemists, engineers, watch and instrument makers and mechanics. Others become doctors, computer experts or psychologists. Whatever the job, their own cars will always be in top shape. It is a matter of course for everything to be spick and span.

As already mentioned, Virgoans are not particularly ambitious and therefore are happier when supervised at work. If attention to detail is required then they are very capable and proficient in problem-solving or working in science or medicine. Although they like to be appreciated, they are happier working as a member of a team. They have an incisive style, useful in the media and the teaching profession.

Health
Virgo rules the abdomen and intestines, and its subjects suffer most commonly from dysentery, colic, diarrhoea, constipation, in digestion and debility. As a general rule, their health is good, though they are prone to worry causelessly over themselves, and to resort to all kinds of patent medicines and quack remedies. A morbid craving for drink or drugs may be experienced, and should be eradicated forthwith.

To attract good vibrations
In order to draw to themselves the right kind of magnetism, those born under Virgo should wear and be surrounded with pale blue, pale gold and yellow. Jade green will also be harmonious, for it is the colour of Mercury.

Wider aspects
There is a desire for purity, perfection and happiness, which, provided that their self-esteem is strong enough, is attainable through application of their own qualities.

Associations
Animal—squirrel.
Birds—parrot, magpie.
Colour—grey, green, brown.

Day—Wednesday.

Flowers— bright small flowers, e.g. buttercup, Madonna lily, cornflower, valerian.

Food—root vegetables.

Gemstone—cornelian, jade, diamond, jasper, sardonyx (a white/brown banded variety of onyx).

Metals—platinum for Virgo; quicksilver for Mercury.

Numbers—ten for Virgo; five for Mercury.

Tree—hazel, nut producing varieties.

Famous Virgos

Ingrid Bergman	Actress
Leonard Bernstein	Composer, conductor
Agatha Christie	Author
Sean Connery	Actor
Jimmy Connors	Tennis player
Roald Dahl	Author
Julio Iglesias	Singer
Lenny Henry	Comedian
Michael Jackson	Rock megastar
Louis XIV	King of France
Sophia Loren	Actress
Leo Tolstoy	Author
Raquel Welch	Actress

Libra

Dates

23 September to 23 October. The Sun enters Libra on September 23, and leaves this sign on approximately October 23. Since the full power of Libra is not exerted until about September 27, when the decreasing influence of Virgo finally ceases, persons born between September 23 and 27 are also partly ruled by Virgo, and they should consult the attributes given by that sign as well.

Origin and glyph

The element of the scales may have several origins, possibly from their use in weighing harvests; the glyph is similar to a yoke.

Ruling planet and groupings

Venus; masculine, cardinal and air.

Typical traits

Librans are true to their origin—they are always trying to achieve a balance, whether between views, negotiating parties, or in their own environment. In many instances, because they prefer not to take one side or the other, they sit in the middle, and this indecision can be their greatest fault. Turned to positive effect, by combining their desire to balance with their undoubted charm, Librans make fine 'diplomats' and can often settle an argument to everyone's satisfaction. They are also easy-going and like quiet surroundings at home or work, but although they may appear vulnerable, they are in fact quite tough and ensure that they follow their own plans.

Libra is an airy sign, and is ruled by the beautiful planet Venus. Its symbol is the scales, typifying balance, justice and harmony, which form the keynote of those born under this sign. Such persons have a natural ability to weigh, compare and estimate facts, and to arrive at an unbiased decision, while it is a remarkable fact that they are able to judge the weight of material objects and can match shades of colour more accurately than people of any other type. Though full of sentiment, they seldom allow their own feelings to interfere with what they consider to be just; and they are broad-minded, tolerant and lenient to the faults of others, realizing that errors and failings are natural to the human race. But they detest injustice, cruelty and unfair treatment, and are always ready to take up arms on behalf of anybody who has been wronged.

In most of the activities of life they are inclined to take a middle course and to avoid extremes of any kind. Under the influence of Venus, the planet of concord and harmony, they constantly crave peace and happy surroundings, and their horror of all strife, worry and unpleasantness makes them invariably pliant, accommodating and complaisant; this trait may easily degenerate into a fault, and it would do the majority of Libra subjects no harm to cultivate some of the tougher moral fibre that distinguishes, for example, natives of Aries and Virgo.

Subjects of Libra are gentle, courteous and affectionate in their manner and speech, and are not easily roused to anger, except by the contemplation of injustice. They cannot maintain a quarrel for long, and seldom feel resentment afterwards. In religious matters they are very tolerant, setting the spirit and relative moral value of any doctrine far above the observance of rites and formulas. They dislike monotony and are fond of change, travelling and seeing interesting and beautiful sights, but if chained by circumstances to one place or occupation, their unfailing good humour enables them to make the best of the situation.

If you suggest to a Libran that it must be much better to live in a town than in the countryside, he or she will immediately start singing the praises of fresh air and healthy country life and how marvellous it is to live somewhere where everyone knows everyone else. And then they'll point out the endless problems of living in a big city with all that traffic, noise and pollution!

You might then propose that it would be wonderful to live in the country, and he or she will then give you a long lecture on how boring it is to live out in the country, where everyone gossips about each other. No, the big city is where the action is, with discos, cinemas and concerts: no time to be bored there!

It is one of the Libran's most typical traits that he or she will always see both sides of a case. This is what makes Librans such good mediators in any quarrel, for even though they love a good discussion they cannot bear disagreements.

Another Libran trait is the ability to go on talking incessantly, or until someone begs them to shut up. But to be fair, they are also good listeners.

Do you think that sounds pretty confusing? Well it is. Librans can be very confusing people. For they are always trying to balance things, to weight the scales evenly. So they can change from being sweet, charming and calm to restless, irritating and stubborn.

Librans often have a weight problem. They love sweet things and find it hard to resist temptation when there are chocolate, sweets or cakes around.

It can sometimes be difficult for people to work out how Librans really feel about things, which is not surprising when they often don't know themselves. Perhaps it's because they try so hard to please others, and are therefore willing to sacrifice their own needs and suppress their own feelings to make others happy

Libra subjects are natural homemakers, and can settle down anywhere, provided their surroundings are congenial; they then hasten to collect around them as many beautiful ornaments, furnishings and other pleasing things as lie within their means.

Intellectually, they are highly developed, and not infrequently of a scholarly turn of mind, with a decided love of the past, which their rich imagination endows with colour and life. However, their tendency to avoid unpleasantness of all kinds may impel them to seek the easiest road through life, with the result that they often turn out indolent and too easy-going, and so neglect and fail to make the best of their fine talents.

Librans are often accused of being lazy, but this is not really justified. If they are interested enough, they will happily work until late at night. But afterwards they sink into a kind of stupor, and wild horses won't get them moving again, especially not to help around the house. They will slouch in front of the TV, or perhaps read a magazine. But then all of a sudden they come to life again and become just as energetic as before.

The strong imagination of Libra folk makes them intuitive, inventive and ingenious, and when their well-balanced reasoning power is added a strong scientific or philosophic genius may be produced. Of this type were Michael Faraday and G. B. Beccaria, the pioneers of electricity; George Westinghouse and Robert Stephenson, the engineers; Noah Webster, the lexicographer; Hugh Miller, the geologist, and Sir Christopher Wren, the famous architect.

Relationships and love

Libra subjects make loyal, cheerful and affectionate friends, who are always ready to put their own interests last. They are, as a rule, probably more happy and contented in marriage than any other type, for their deep fund of affection triumphs over difficulties and conflicts of temperament that would wreck the majority of marriages.

Good friends are often born under the same sign, or at

any rate belong to the same element. Libra is an air sign, so this means that Librans get on well with the other air signs, Aquarius and Gemini.

Librans always want to do others a good turn, but they also care about other people's opinions of them. So they risk acquiring friends who really only want to exploit their kindness. Librans find it hard to distinguish between true and false friends, so they sometimes experience terrible disappointments in their relationships.

They tend to look for friends among the smartest and most popular people, because they are so unsure of their own feelings. These are usually only superficial friendships but if Librans manage to find true friends, they can be relied on to be faithful, considerate and keen to preserve their friendships.

In relationships with a partner, Librans can be complete romantics and regard this relationship as very important, so much so that even the Libran indecisiveness can be overcome for a time. They tend to fit well into the domestic scene, being quite capable of organizing the household with their usual equable approach to all things, including money.

If you are a girl who has fallen for a Libran, do not expect him to rush up and invite you to go to the cinema. No, you might as well jump in at the deep end and ask him out instead. And you need not fear that he'll feel that you have offended him by taking the initiative. On the contrary, he will just be grateful that he has been spared the job of making a decision.

Librans of both sexes are very romantic. And they set great store by everything being perfect. So the first time you invite your friend home to tea, do not offer him milk from a carton or bottle, but try to borrow a tea-set with a proper jug and sugar bowl.

Librans do not like being alone and love to have someone

to look after and care for. But they often find it difficult to understand their own feelings and may therefore mistake friendship for love.

They are prone to jealousy and want you all to themselves. Watch out, otherwise you may lose all your other friends.

It can be hard work having a Libran sweetheart, because they are so romantic and expect you to live up to their ideals.

When Librans fall in love seriously, they will do anything for their beloved. They make so many sacrifices that it can end up having a stifling effect on their partner. So it is important to stress that the Libran must learn to satisfy their own needs as well.

Librans make kind parents, although they must ensure that they are strong-willed and insist upon children doing as they are told. The Libran indecision might irritate some children, and every effort should be made to answer a child's queries.

The most congenial types to mate with Libra people are those born between January 21 and February 21 and between May 21 and June 21.

Children

Children with this Sun sign tend to be charming and affable, and are often popular at school. Indecision and laziness should be identified and wherever possible overcome.

Librans are usually very tidy people. A Libran child will even offer to clean up at home, if the place looks too messy. So Librans are often spoiled rotten by their parents, who think they are such easy children.

Because Librans are often spoiled at home, they can be impossible in Kindergarten or when they start school, since they are used to being the centre of attention and getting their own way. But if they had a sensible upbringing, they will be a treat for their teachers, as they are very keen on learning and love discussing.

Good advice

As already mentioned, Librans are willing to suppress their own needs in order to satisfy those of other people. But sometimes it is all just too much for them and they become absolutely furious, perhaps with the wrong people. If you are a Libran, you should learn to say no when necessary. You will be a lot happier yourself, and in the long term you will get on better with others, because they will respect you more.

Air and earth compatibility

People born under an air sign or an earth sign often find it hard to get on. The first category dream up airy plans and ideas, and cannot understand why the more down-to-earth Virgos or Capricorns do not immediately fall for their crazy ideas.

They will, however, be able to cooperate on individual projects where, for example, the thoroughness and methodical nature of the Taurean will harmonise well with the imagination of the Libran. But as soon as one of them tries to take on the dominating role, they are asking for trouble and the friendship may collapse.

Of all the earth signs, Librans get on best with Taurus.

Air and fire compatibility

Air nourishes fire and fans its flames even higher. And the warmth of the fire makes the air rise.

So it would seem that these two signs are compatible and can offer mutual support. On the other hand these two signs often lose touch with reality when they discuss their ambitious plans.

Of the fire signs, Librans get on best with Leos and Sagittarians.

Air and water compatibility

You cannot breathe under water, so a water sign can have a suffocating effect on a Libran. On the other hand a Scorpion or a Cancerian may be able to teach the Libran to understand and handle his feelings better.

Of all the water signs, Librans get on best with Pisceans.

Occupations

As mentioned, the tact and evenhandedness of Librans make them ideal as diplomats, in public relations, or any profession requiring these qualities. Their appreciation of art and beauty lends itself to a career in the arts or literature, and fashion, beauty and related professions are all possibilities for them. Although they like to work with other people, especially those of a like mind, they are sufficiently ambitious to reach for the top, although any isolation that this might produce would be unwelcome.

Being apt at learning, adaptable, level-headed and capable of calm decision, Libra subjects can make a success of almost any career. Preferably, however, they should follow some line in which their strong artistic tastes and good sense of proportion have full scope. Thus they make excellent artists, musicians, writers, poets, sculptors, landscape gardeners, florists, and dress designers. Others will seek to develop the Libran interest in people and become health workers or psychologists. As a general rule, they work better when in employment or partnership than when alone. They often find a talent for the law, and their strong judicial powers may carry them to great heights The gift of cool and rapid decision imparted by Libra has also produced many great naval and military commanders, including Augustus Caesar, Pompey, Lord Clive, Lord Nelson, Lord Collingwood, Frederick III of Germany, Lord Roberts, and Marshal Foch.

Health
Libra rules the kidneys, lumbar regions and skin, and its subjects are liable to suffer from disorders affecting these parts, such Bright's disease, nephritis, diabetes, eczema and skin eruptions. Their nerves, also, are liable to be overstrained, and they should avoid worry and depression of spirits.

To attract good vibrations
Blue and violet are the colours that accord best with Libra, and they should be used freely in order to attract harmonious astral vibrations.

Wider aspects
Librans work well anywhere where there are pleasant surroundings that are well ordered.

Associations
Animals—hart, bear.
Bird—dove.
Colour—blues and pinks.
Day—Friday.
Flowers—bluebells, violet, white rose, large roses.
Food—cereals, most fruits and spices.
Gemstones—sapphire, opal for Libra, lapis lazuli for Venus, its ruler.
Metal—copper.
Numbers—eight for Libra; six for Venus.
Trees—ash, apple, almond, walnut.

Famous Librans

Julie Andrews	Actress
Sebastian Coe	Athlete
Graham Greene	Novelist
Felicity Kendal	Actress
John Lennon	Singer
Roger Moore	Actor
Martina Navratilova	Tennis player
Horatio Nelson	Naval commander
Oscar Wilde	Playwright
Sir Christopher Wren	Architect
Luciano Pavarotti	Tenor

Scorpio

129

Dates

24 October to 22 November. The Sun enters Scorpio on or about October 24 each year, and leaves it approximately on November 22. Persons born between October 24 and 27 are, however, also ruled to some extent by the preceding sign, Libra, whose influence does not die away entirely until the latter date.

Origin and glyph

The origin of the scorpion is unknown, although it appears in numerous guises in ancient history. The glyph symbolizes a serpent's coil and is linked with the male genitalia.

Ruling planet and groupings

Pluto; feminine, fixed and water.

Typical traits

Scorpians can show rather a mix of behaviour and character, on the one hand being very determined and strong-willed, and on the other being obsessive, awkward and arrogant. Once committed to something, whether a person or an ideal, they will be very faithful, although they are susceptible to being melodramatic, and when emotions become involved logic suffers. They are usually energetic, wanting the most out of life, whether at work or play, and will not relinquish their goal easily. Although they are perfectly capable of sacrificing others, they do hold on to what is right and will exhibit a strong sense of fair play and reason.

Scorpio, whose symbol is the stinging scorpion, is a negative and watery sign, but is ruled by the fiery planet Mars. Its subjects are a mass of extremes and contradictions, and even at the best are always difficult to size up or classify. Powerfully magnetic, brimful of energy, intense in their emotions, and subtle and involved in their actions and manner of thought, they have perhaps the strongest personalities of all the zodiacal types. The willpower which their can exert over other people is enormous. Not only by their gift of rhetoric—in which they excel—but by means of something far deeper, some strange psychological power, they can mould and twist other people to their will, either individually or in the mass.

Most people do not like losing at games, but if you meet someone who considers any defeat to be a total catastrophe, that person will probably turn out to be a Scorpio. Scorpions hate to lose.

Scorpions also hate false modesty, so if you ask one whether they are good at something or other and they think they are, they will say so straight out. And if you want their opinion about your latest hairstyle or boyfriend, you will get an equally honest answer. Scorpions will not resort to flattery just to obtain something. That is beneath their dignity.

Some people are too embarrassed to admit that they are Scorpions, because the Scorpion is a creature who attacks his victim and kills it with the poison sitting in its tail. If it finds itself cornered it will even turn its poison onto itself.

But there really is no reason to be ashamed about being a Scorpion. A Scorpion who has had a loving home will develop into a friendly, caring person.

Scorpions are incredibly inquisitive. For instance they want to know what other people are thinking, and they will go on asking until they get an answer. And there is no point in trying to fool a Scorpion, because they will see through any deception straight away.

Scorpio people are nearly always inclined to be haughty, vain, and self-satisfied, and often nourish for their associates a contempt which they do not hesitate to display in harsh and biting words. They often seem to be possessed with a demon of perversity, and they love to impress and 'shock' people by some dramatic and unexpected action, usually of an unpleasant nature.

They have amazing powers of tenacity and resistance, and are seldom discouraged when their plans go awry and success seems far away. They will meet the most crushing blows without cringing or changing expression; in fact, they always know when and how to conceal their emotions, although there are few people who live on their emotions so much as those born under Scorpio.

Idealists and humanitarians at heart, the more developed types among these subjects are ever eager to defend and champion the weak and oppressed; but they often speak slightingly of those whom they uphold and protect, and affect a contempt of charity and kind actions! Naturally gifted with dramatic ability, many of them act throughout their daily life and, in a spirit of perversity, seem anxious to give the world an entirely wrong impression of their character and temperament. They have little use for convention, and often fly deliberately in the face of established custom and propriety, a course which seems to afford them keen pleasure.

Scorpions have good memories, and will remember your kindnesses as well as your cruelties. Your generosity will be richly rewarded, but you can expect dreadful revenge to be taken if you have been nasty. Just try to make fun of a Scorpion in public and you will find that you will receive a dose of your own medicine—with interest.

They are hard workers and never spare themselves, and if they are gifted with ambition—as is usually the case nothing can stand in the way of its realization. They lay their plans with calm deliberation, meet and overcome obstacles with the greatest coolness and ingenuity, and often look upon other people as pawns to be sacrificed to their own success.

Natives of Scorpio often have pronounced psychic gifts, and feel drawn towards a study of the occult. Many of them can sublimate their intense vital force into religion or mysticism, and this process produces personalities which are outstanding and unique. As examples we may cite Saint Augustine, William Cowper and Samuel Taylor Coleridge, the poets, and Alexander I, tsar of Russia, each of whom had a pronounced strain of mysticism in his or her nature.

A notable person born under Scorpio is usually remarkable in many other ways than that in which his or her particular talent or genius has distinguished him or her; he or she is the sort of man who is fated to make his or her mark in the world, no matter how he or she chooses to do so. This strength of character is observable in Theodore Roosevelt, Captain Cook, Danton, Gambetta, Franz Liszt, Benvenuto Cellini, Martin Luther, Edward VII and William Hogarth, all of whom were born under the rays of Scorpio.

Relationships and love

Those born under Scorpio have an intense love nature, which, if they value their happiness, they must not allow to get beyond control. They should guard against sudden and impulsive attachments that have no basis of real affection. Scorpio subjects are critical and not easy to please, and are liable to become violently jealous with little or no cause, but they may be successfully handled by a tactful partner who knows, and allows for, all the vagaries of their strong personality.

The Scorpian's desire to stay with a relationship holds good for partnerships, although their energy may need to be channelled if it is not to prove disruptive. They prefer people who are equally strong-willed but, despite outward appearances, may themselves be weaker than they look. They are certainly prone to depression, from which they find it hard to emerge, and this may contribute to the apparent extremes in marriage—some are very good, others less so.

If you are a man who has attracted a Scorpio woman, you must be someone really special. Because she will not settle for any old Tom, Dick or Harry. And if you break up, your next girlfriend will have quite a lot to live up to because Scorpions are never boring companions. They are very emotional and when they fall in love they do so with such ardour that it can quite take one's breath away.

But there is also a reverse side to their emotions. Scorpions get jealous very quickly, and their anger will erupt like a volcano if they have even the slightest suspicion that you have been flirting with somebody else. And even if you are quite innocent, the suspicion can be so powerful that it will break up your relationship.

Scorpions love to be in control of their lives. They want to run everything themselves, even their love lives. You must expect that your Scorpion sweetheart will want to satisfy his or her own needs first before considering yours. But once committed, he or she will be extra sweet and loving.

Good friends are often born under the same Sun sign, or at any rate belong to the same element. Scorpio is a water sign, so this means that Scorpions get on well with other water signs, Pisces and Cancer.

Scorpions often do not have a lot of friends, because they are very fussy and can easily see through people. On the other hand, once you have been accepted by a Scorpion, he or she will become a very faithful friend.

If you are friends with a Scorpion, do not expect to keep many secrets. For instance, if you have fallen for the new person in your class, it will not be long before your Scorpio friend has sussed it out. He or she is not only good at guessing other people's feelings, but is also extremely inquisitive.

But do not try to stick your nose too deeply into the Scorpion's private life. Scorpions do not like that at all. For as much as they like to guess your secrets, they want to guard their own.

As parents they will do their utmost for their offspring, but they can push a little too much and should consciously develop a balanced approach to parenthood, allowing their children some freedom.

Their closest affinities are formed with people born between February 21 and March 21 and between June 21 and July 21.

Children

Some children are often very affectionate but equally prone to sudden tempers. They should be helped to talk over problems to avoid depressed silences, and their emotional energies should be diverted into productive occupations.

Scorpion children love dangerous games, and so they inevitably have accidents. But they are not cowards and they don't howl or scream if they have to have a cut cleaned or a couple of stitches.

Scorpio children love monsters and horror films, and they prefer ghost stories to fairy tales any day.

As Scorpions hate to lose, they also try to be amongst the best at school. They have a lot of energy and really make an effort to attain the goals they have set themselves.

Scorpions tend to be extremist. No-one can hate as much as a Scorpion who feels that he or she has been victimized. And problems may arise in school if the Scorpion gets on the wrong side of teachers or friends. But Scorpions are also willing to go through hell and high water for those they like.

Good advice

Scorpio people would do both themselves and others a favour if they learned to control their tempers. That goes for when they are playing games and think they are about to lose, as well as when they think they have been unfairly treated by others.

Water and air compatibility

The air signs, Gemini, Libra and Aquarius, can learn a lot from the water signs, and vice versa. For example, Scorpions find it hard to grasp that other people are different to them and don't think the way they do. Air sign people are much more understanding. But water sign people can teach air sign people to recognise their own emotions.

Water and air get on well with each other, but just as water can have a suffocating effect on air, for you cannot breathe under water, a Scorpion can be so dominating that an air sign person feels stifled.

On the other hand, the air can whip up great storms and high seas. And this can happen if an Aquarian or a Libran is not sufficiently aware of Scorpion sensitivity, which may provoke a Scorpion tempest.

Of all the air signs, Scorpions get on best with Geminis.

Water and earth compatibility

Water is necessary for all growth on earth.

This means that people born under an earth sign usually get on well with Scorpions. Earth sign people are down-to-earth and sensible, and Scorpions are more emotional. So if they do not pressurise each other too much but respect each other's idosyncrasies, they can derive much pleasure from each other.

But just as a plant will wilt and die if it is not watered, a friendship will also flounder if the Scorpion gives free rein to his emotions without showing consideration for his more down-to-earth Taurean friends.

Of all the earth signs, Scorpions usually get on best with Capricorns or Virgos.

Water and fire compatibility

These two signs are not normally well suited. Water puts

out fire. Scorpions just cannot cope with an Arian or a Leo who comes charging in with some half-baked project to be carried out right away.

In return, fire sign people are irritated by the thoroughness and systematic nature of the Scorpions.

Occupations

Both Scorpio and its ruler, Mars, favour success in the army and navy. Other congenial careers include those of government official, overseer, magistrate, butcher, iron-founder, brazier, brewer, chemist, photographer, and dentist, while the most skilful of surgeons are produced by this sign. A love of secrecy and intrigue is inherent in the Scorpio nature, and this may produce excellent detectives, spies and secret service agents, as well as prominent Freemasons and members of secret societies.

They do not always aspire to the top jobs at work. But they do like to be in control and so they prefer to pull the strings and direct things the way they want.

Scorpions are also attracted by danger in their choice of jobs. Many of them attempt to realise their childhood dreams and end up as soldiers, policemen or firemen.

But their great interest in other people's emotional lives also leads them to jobs as psychologists, lawyers or social workers.

When running a business, a Scorpian will work to his or her very limit to help ensure success and, to a certain extent, they welcome challenges and problems. They can employ charm when necessary but can also be hard and demanding at times. They also like financial security and are willing to work for it. Scorpians are well suited to being in the medical profession or in a profession where analysis and research are required.

To attract good vibrations

The deeper shades of red harmonize best with Scorpio, and russet-brown is also beneficial. These colours should be incorporated in the clothes of Scorpio subjects, and in their household decorations, in order to attract the maximum of good fortune.

Wider aspects:

The character of a Scorpian is built up of a fine balance of attributes, which, in a positive sense, can yield a tremendous achiever but conversely may produce someone riven with jealousy.

Associations

Animals—wolf and panther.
Birds—eagle and vulture.
Colour—deep red.
Day—Tuesday.
Flowers—heather and chrysanthemum, dark red flowers such as geraniums.
Food—foods with strong flavours.
Gemstones—opal, all red stones are beneficial, especially the ruby; also beryl, topaz and turquoise.
Metal—iron.
Number—nine for both Scorpio and Mars, its ruler.
Trees—thorn-bearing varieties.

Famous Scorpions

Boris Becker	Tennis player
Georges Bizet	Composer
Richard Burton	Actor
Prince Charles	Prince of Wales
John Cleese	Comedian

Captain James Cook	Explorer
Marie Curie	Physicist
Bob Hoskins	Actor
Mahalia Jackson	Gospel singer
Grace Kelly	Actress
Burt Lancaster	Actor
Claude Monet	Painter
Theodore Roosevelt	US president
Leon Trotsky	Communist leader
Jan Vermeer	Painter

Sagittarius

Dates

23 November to 21 December. The Sun enters the zodiacal sign Sagittarius about November 23, to leave it a month later, about December 21. However, the full power of Sagittarius does not begin to take effect until about November 27, for until that date the influence of Scorpio is also active, though declining. Hence, persons born between November 23 and 27 are partly ruled by Scorpio, and should consult the properties of that sign as well as those of Sagittarius.

Origin and glyph

The origin is unknown, but the glyph, represents the arrow of the Centaur.

Ruling planet and groupings

Jupiter, masculine, mutable and fire.

Typical traits

Sagittarians are essentially gregarious, friendly and enthusiastic, with a desire to achieve all goals that are set. They are rarely beset by depression, but their inborn enthusiasm can sometimes take them too far, and they may take risks. Although they are versatile and intelligent, their desire to jump from the task in hand to the next may result in some tasks being unfinished. In excess, their good qualities can become a nuisance, leading to tactless, hurtful comments (without the intent to hurt) and jokes that go too far.

Sagittarius is the third of the fiery signs, and is symbolized by an archer, or a centaur, drawing his or her bow. In magnetism it is positive, and it is under the rule of the benign and expansive planet Jupiter. Natives of this sign are distinguished by frankness, sincerity and optimism; they have a strongly developed sense of justice, and are tolerant, philanthropic and humane. They display great sympathy with human nature, and are generous and charitable to a degree. They like being made a repository of other people's troubles, and are very fond of giving advice, but are apt to become sententious and patronizing, which often lessens the appreciation of their kindness. They are intensely hard workers, though in the pursuit of their aims they are apt to run along a somewhat narrow track, so that much escapes their notice that might be helpful to them.

They are very sociable, and are popular in friendly and convivial gatherings, though they are apt to affront their individual friends by their extreme outspokenness. They are essentially honest and hate deception and trickery in any form, and usually they lead very respectable lives and bow unfailingly to convention. Always ready, and even anxious, to shoulder responsibilities, they are solicitous in their regard for the welfare of those under their tutelage or in their employ.

Being gifted with considerable strength of will, they show great independence and insist on conducting their affairs and living their lives in their own way. They are both versatile and impulsive, and therefore frequently make sudden decisions or change their occupations or interests in a totally unexpected way.

Many people born under Sagittarius are deeply religious, and their faith in moral and spiritual matters seldom falters. Others are fond of philosophizing, and in this direction often display great depth of thought. Examples of the highest type of keen and philosophic intellect given by Sagittarius can be seen in John Milton, Thomas Carlyle, Jonathan Swift and Heinrich Heine.

Sagittarians are strangely prone to theorize and make shrewd guesses as to the outcome of events. Indeed, their intuition and foresight are often considerable, and reliance upon them is amply justified by the success achieved by the higher types of Sagittarians when guided by their own impulses. Many Sagittarius folk display the curious characteristic of completely altering their occupation or habits of life, quite irrespective of advancing age, change of abode and other circumstances, and often without any obvious motive at all; and they are quite as sincere and successful in this new existence as they were in the former. A few notable Sagittarians in whom this peculiarity may be observed are General Monk, who achieved fame first as an able general and then crowned it by restoring the supremacy of England on the sea; Prince Rupert, the dashing cavalry commander, who later became an admiral and eventually retired to the seclusion of the chemical laboratory; and Thomas Becket and Lope de Vega, the Spanish dramatist, both men of pleasure who became rigid ascetics.

Sagittarians are very often of athletic build, with long and well-developed legs, and they are extremely fond of sport; they are at their happiest in the open air and in the company of dogs and horses.

Sagittarians are restless. They hate sitting or standing still. They love fast cars, dangerous jobs and violent sports.

There is an old saying that truth comes from the mouths of babes. It also could be said about Sagittarians. Not because they want to be outspoken, but rather because they are slightly naive and just cannot imagine that others could be offended or hurt by their remarks. They are often rather tactless but in fact think themselves to be very diplomatic.

Sagittarians are prone to very erratic moods. One moment they are floating on cloud nine and feel they are totally in control. And then, if they are given a lot of boring tasks to do, they will suddenly become fed up. If they are able to pass their work on to others, they will do so quite readily.

Sagittarians often have money problems. They behave as though money grows on trees, and they get very annoyed when they discover that it doesn't.

The undeveloped types of Sagittarians are inclined to be pretentious, vain and patronizing. They love to make a parade of any generous actions which they may be called upon to perform, and are full of religious cant and smug self-satisfaction. They do not hesitate to commit the meanest of actions, and are quite unscrupulous in the pursuit of their ambitions; but they endeavour to conceal the unpleasant side of their nature with a cloak of hypocrisy and bluff, for the good opinion of the world is very precious to them.

Relationships and love

Sagittarians have a great capacity for friendship, and are popular among their associates, but they are apt to lose friends through want of tact. They make good husbands, wives and parents, who never shirk the responsibilities of family life, but they often marry unhappily, probably being carried away by a passing impulse. However, their proud and independent spirit can be depended upon to hide their unhappiness from the eyes of the world, and they will endeavour to make the best of things in order to preserve appearances. They are fond of home life, and take a great pride in the comfort and adornment of their home.

Freedom is important to Sagittarians, so much so that it may inhibit long-term relationships. After settling down, however, they are good in the family context, and their enthusiasm can help lift boredom or depression. Sagittarians will enjoy a friendship or partnership more if they are given a loose rein to enable them to do what they want. Often their ultimate goal is not materialistic but more spiritual.

Sagittarians have a strong sense of independence, so it is not easy to trap one. This is not because the male Sagittarian does not like women, on the contrary, but that doesn't mean having to be tied hand and foot to one.

If you are a woman who has fallen for a Sagittarian, and he suggests you go on a camping tour together, don't for one minute believe that he is a boy scout. He may have very different plans in mind, so you had better 'be prepared'!

Sagittarians find it hard to talk about or to display their feelings, so if you fall in love with one, do not expect to spend your evenings together holding hands and discussing your beautiful future. But you definitely will not be bored.

Good friends are often born under the same Sun sign, or at any rate belong to the same element. Sagittarius is a fire sign, so this means that Sagittarians get on well with the other fire signs, Aries and Leo.

Sagittarians usually have lots of friends, because they are so honest about their feelings and opinions. And even though some people may be taken aback by the Sagittarian's outspoken remarks, they soon realise that these are never ill-meant.

Sagittarians are not easily offended, perhaps because they are both optimistic and somewhat naive. If friends try to play a trick on a Sagittarian, say by sending a box full of polystyrene chips, the Sagittarian will not be upset, but simply believe that they forgot to include the present.

Sagittarians make exciting friends, because there is usually something happening when they are around. They are always hatching some plot, and even though this may seem quite daft, Lady Luck seems to be on their side, and they succeed where others would fail. This could be because they have total faith in their own ideas.

Sagittarians love to talk and discuss things with their friends, but if the conversation gets too close to the subject of emotions, especially their own, they immediately try to change the subject.

As parents, their approach to life means that they encourage their children to be outgoing, and this is fine providing a child is not nervous or shy.

Sagittarius folk mate most harmoniously with those born between March 21 and April 21, and between July 21 and August 21.

Children

Sagittarian children are very inquisitive. They are always asking questions. And when their poor parents finally yell out "I don't want to hear that word 'why' again", they will inevitably reply "Why not?".

Sagittarians can also drive their parents crazy in other ways. They hate any routine jobs such as tidying up and cleaning their rooms. Of course there are many other Sun signs who share this trait, but the Sagittarian is by far the worst in this respect.

Sagittarians do not have a strong sense of family. They tend to seek their independence and move away from home very early. Sometimes they move far away, because they love to travel. They soon tire of any humdrum domesticity and are always on the go.

Sagittarians are usually clumsy, and that goes both for when they make some remark which can hurt others and when they walk down the street. Parents of Sagittarians need a well-stocked first aid box, because their offspring often have accidents.

Sagittarians are usually happy and content with life. Their endless curiosity makes them ideal pupils, but only if the teachers make the lessons exciting and interesting. Old fashioned discipline or boring teachers just produce apathy and indifference in the Sagittarians, and nor are they too fond of homework.

Their endless questioning can also drive their teachers round the bend. And the teachers really need to know their stuff if they are to be a match for a Sagittarius.

The natural enthusiasm of Sagittarian children should be guided to productive ends, and their instinctive dislike of rules should be dealt with diplomatically. There is considerable potential in the child who has a gentle guiding hand upon him or her.

Good advice

Because of their tendency to leave the more boring, everyday tasks to others, Sagittarians are often accused of being lazy and self-centred. So they would be well advised to realise that you have to learn to take the rough with the smooth.

With their lack of economic sense, adult Sagittarians would do well either to leave money matters to their partners or to make a conscious effort to change their attitude.

Fire and earth compatibility

There is nothing as annoying as someone saying "Stop making such a fuss", when you have pulled out all the stops to convince them of your brilliant idea. Or who just reacts to your grand plans with some derisive remark.

People born under a fire sign often lack respect and understanding for the world in which they find themselves. "It'll work out" they say, and run the sort of risks that a Virgo or a Capricorn wouldn't dream of. But these two signs can learn a lot from each other. The Sagittarian could do with a bit of common sense and thoroughness, whilst people born under an earth sign could benefit from following their hearts sometimes, not just their minds.

Of all the earth signs, Sagittarians get on best with Taurus.

Fire and air compatibility

While an earth sign can have a suffocating effect on a fire sign like Sagittarius, the air signs fan their flames so they burn even brighter. And the strong sense of independence which they share creates a mutual attraction, though usually more as friends than as partners.

However, they may lose touch with reality, and the grand plans which a Sagittarian and Aquarian cook up together could end up as nothing more than hot air.

Of the air signs, Sagittarians get on best with Aquarians and Librans.

Fire and water compatibility

People born under these two signs find it hard to understand each other, and thus a Sagittarian will rarely count a Scorpio or a Piscean amongst his or her best friends.

Sagittarians are in too much of a hurry to make allowances for the water sign people, whom they consider to be too 'wet', and too timid to take a risk now and again. On the other hand the water sign people think that the Sagittarian's plans are too risky for their taste.

Of all the water signs, Sagittarians get on best with Cancerians.

Occupations

Sagittarians are naturally fitted for positions of authority in which their advice, aid and judgment can be sought by others. Thus they excel in medicine, the law and the Church, and as employers of labour, naval and military officers, technical experts of all kinds, politicians, missionaries, relieving officers, inspectors, nurses, matrons, modistes and officials of charitable organizations. Many veterinary surgeons and dealers in dogs and horses are found under this sign.

They often have a deep love of music and make excellent musicians. In this connection it is interesting to note that the great Beethoven was born under Sagittarius, as also were Weber, Rubinstein, Edward McDowell and Sir Hamilton Harty.

Sagittarians usually have lots of interests, but they are all designed to satisfy their drive for excitement and exploration. Adventures such as mountain-climbing or parachuting are ways of testing their own limits.

Sagittarians may look for a career to satisfy their insatiable curiosity. But as they are also individualistic, they prefer to work on their own. Law and education are areas which many Sagittarians like. But deep down they may dream of becoming astronauts.

Sagittarians are not interested primarily in material gain and because they are particularly interested in education and travel, that is where money may be spent. Work of a varied nature is preferred, but care should be taken to make sure details are not omitted in the race to move on to something new. There is a natural desire to help others, which may manifest itself in a career in teaching, counselling, lecturing, the Church, law, and publishing.

Health

The hips, thighs, nerves and arteries are under the rule of Sagittarius, and its subjects may suffer from rheumatism in the lower limbs, as well as from sciatica, gout and nervous disorders. The lungs and throat may be delicate, and the native may be prone to bronchitis and lung troubles. The commonest accidents suffered by Sagittarians are those affecting the lower limbs, such as sprains, dislocation of the hip and fracture of the thigh.

To attract good vibrations

Orange is the colour most in tune with the vibrations of Sagittarius, while mauve and purple harmonize best with Jupiter, its ruler. Good fortune should ensue if these colours are freely used.

Wider aspects

When both mind and body have a certain degree of freedom, Sagittarians are at their best and will then employ their versatility and intellectual strengths to the full.

Associations

Animal—horse.
Bird—eagle.
Colour—purple, deep blue.
Day—Thursday.
Flowers—carnations and wallflowers.
Food—good food is enjoyed but overindulgence should be avoided. Specifically currants and the onion family.
Gemstones—sapphire for Sagittarius; amethyst for Jupiter, topaz.
Metal—tin.
Numbers—four for Sagittarius; three for Jupiter.
Trees—oak, ash, mulberry, vine and birch.

Famous Sagittarians

Woody Allen	Comedian, writer, film director
Ludwig van Beethoven	Composer
Kenneth Branagh	Actor
Ronnie Corbett	Comedian
Noel Coward	Playwright
Walt Disney	Film producer
Jane Fonda	Actress
Gilbert O'Sullivan	Singer
Frank Sinatra	Singer, actor
Steven Spielberg	Film director
Henri Toulouse-Lautrec	Painter

Capricorn

Dates

22 December to 20 January. The Sun passes into Capricorn on approximately December 22 and leaves it about January 20. People born on the cusp of the sign—between December 22 and 27—are, however, also influenced to some extent by the gradually declining power of the preceding sign, Sagittarius, and they should consult the qualities given by this sign as well as those with which Capricorn endows them.

Origin and glyph

It may have originated with a mythical sea-goat from ancient Babylon. The glyph, is said to represent a goat's head and a fish's tail.

Ruling planet and groupings

Saturn, feminine, cardinal and earth.

Typical traits

It is said that there are two types of Capricornian, one of which has greater and higher hopes of life. In general, they are patient, practical and can be very shy, preferring to stay in the background—but, they are strong-willed and can stand up for themselves. Capricornians have a reputation for being mean, ambitious and rather hard people. A mean streak may often be directed at the self, and ambition, if tempered with realism and humour, can be positive. Usually the character is enhanced by other elements of the chart to produce a warmer personality.

Capricorn is an earthy sign, and is ruled by the secretive and restraining planet Saturn. The symbol of Capricorn is the goat, an animal which delights in climbing the highest mountains and the most precipitous rocks. Even so do the patient, persistent and dogged subjects of Capricorn seek the steepest and most arduous paths through life to reach the summit of their worldly ambition or spiritual salvation. Hard work, fatigue, and self-denial are counted as nothing, and all their energies are bent towards one object. Practical, shrewd, and calculating, and of a grave, self-contained disposition, they scorn all forms of extravagance and display and all unnecessary expenditure of energy. They are reserved, secretive and taciturn, and very averse to taking anybody into their confidence or imparting their thoughts and opinions to those around them.

Capricornians scorn effusiveness and are unmoved by flattery, and they seldom express wonderment or surprise; but they are amid of knowledge in all its branches, are keenly interested in science and philosophy, and are impelled towards the study of all that is ancient, such as archaeology, history and folklore. They are painstaking and methodical in all they do, and although their researches may be animated by enthusiasm, this is of a quiet and prosaic order and is seldom revealed. Johann Kepler and Sir Isaac Newton, both subjects of Capricorn, are excellent examples of this patient, undemonstrative, but indefatigable spirit of inquiry.

Natives of Capricorn are quick to take the lead in their particular sphere of activity, and their right to do so is usually accepted without question, for their implicit faith in their own powers is rapidly communicated to those about them. If baulked of a position of authority and obliged to work under the domination of others, they become gloomy, morose and mordantly critical.

Though most of them are strongly material, many Capricornians are also idealists at heart, and their love of moral and intellectual freedom often impels them to back up an apparently worthy but hopeless or unpopular cause, even though it is plain that their own interests may suffer thereby. This type of idealism, in a greater or less degree, may be observed in Joan of Arc, Edmund Burke, Alexander Hamilton, Marshal Ney, W. E. Gladstone, President Woodrow Wilson and David Lloyd George, all of whom, at some period of their life fought for their convictions in a difficult or apparently losing battle.

The image of the mountain goat or Capricorn climbing up to the highest peaks also fits the human Capricorn, who sets his or her sights high and is prepared to undertake the long climb upwards to reach his or her goal.

In other words, Capricorns are the ambitious types. They are persevering and patient, and don't mind waiting to fulfil their goal.

Capricorns admire competent and successful people. So they are sometimes regarded as snobs. In turn they often feel that other people are slightly superficial and stupid, but they will not express this opinion in public. There is no point in creating enemies!

Capricorns tend to be pessimists and never embark on any risky or dangerous venture, believing it is bound to fail. They frown on those who take risks and who refuse to plan their lives down to the last detail. But they also tend to become envious when they see how lucky other people can be.

Natives of Capricorn are not easily roused to anger, but, on the other hand, they are very slow to forgive, often nourishing their wrongs in secret for years until the time is ripe for the revenge which they never hesitate to reap in full measure, since they are vindictive beyond the ordinary. They are also inclined to be jealous, suspicious and morose. Extreme melancholy and depression of spirits are perhaps the worst enemies of the Capricorn type, and may colour all their thoughts and actions. Edgar Allan Poe is a striking example of this type, as is also, though in a lesser degree, Thomas Gray, author of the *Elegy Written in a Country Churchyard*.

When badly developed, they may become the most hateful of mankind—timid, callous, tyrannical, intensely selfish, miserly, morbid, lustful, and full of low cunning and duplicity. The superior types are, however, among the noblest members of the human race.

Relationships and love

Subjects of Capricorn make good and true friends, though they are bitter and implacable enemies. In love and marriage, they are capable of deep and passionate affection, though no type is more undemonstrative. They are advised not to marry young, such marriages often proving unfortunate. Much domestic friction can be avoided if they will contrive to overcome their selfishness and cultivate good humour and cheerfulness.

Capricornians make good partners, although they may come late to marriage to ensure a career has been established and that the correct choice is being made. Once set up, they are likely to be happy and to provide well, if economically, for the family. This aspect of caring can extend well outside the immediate family, and although there may be a lack of confidence, a Capricorn subject will not allow him or herself to be pushed around.

Love

A Capricorn always thinks everything over carefully before taking action, and that goes for love affairs too. Like everything else, love is a serious matter, not to be trifled with by simply giving way to one's feelings!

If you fall in love with a Capricorn and manage to get off with him, do not expect him to be romantic. You will not be invited for an expensive meal or be showered with red roses for no particular reason.

If you take the initiative and invite a Capricorn home for

a romantic dinner by candlelight, do not be surprised if he or she turns all the lights on before sitting down to eat. After all, you need to see what you are eating, don't you?

On the other hand, once a Capricorn has found his or her true love, he or she will be very faithful.

If you have a Capricorn boyfriend, do not attempt to show up on the beach topless. He hates causing a stir.

If you have a Capricorn girlfriend, you will do your cause no good if you start making fun of her. She will probably not appreciate the joke, and will definitely not be amused. Nor does she like the type who pretends to be a regular Don Juan and charm the pants off all the girls. She generally prefers the more stable type who keeps a check on both his finances and his love life.

Good friends are often born under the same sign, or at any rate belong to the same element. And as Capricorn is an earth sign, this means that Capricorns get on well with the other earth signs, Virgo and Taurus.

Capricorns are often loners. When they are young they tend to be very serious and think that their peers are either too childish or too irresponsible. They feel that others should concern themselves with the future instead of larking around. And they cannot stand their wild ideas and plans.

Capricorns become more relaxed as they grow older, so by the time they are old, they tend to think their peers are too old for them! And, contrary to most other people, they do not make friends at work, but rather stick to their own or their spouse's families.

Never be disparaging about a Capricorn's family. That makes a Capricorn really mad, and he or she will take immediate offence.

But if you should manage to make friends with a Capricorn, he or she will be a very loyal and faithful friend, who will be prepared to help you when you are in need.

As parents, they can be too strict. However, they encourage their children and will make sacrifices to assist their child's progress.

Those most in harmony with the Capricorn type, both in friendship and marriage, are born between April 21 and May 21 and between August 21 and September 21.

Children

It is said that Capricorns are born old and die young. They have few friends, because most people find them precocious. They in turn think that others are very childish. Try talking about farm animals with a three year-old Capricorn, and he will laugh at you if you say baa-baa instead of sheep.

Capricorn children may be a little slow to develop but usually come into their own eventually. They are very loyal and benefit from a secure background, which offers discipline, but at the same time they should be helped to build up their self-confidence.

On the other hand, Capricorns will still be out mountain climbing or skiing when their contemporaries can barely manage to crawl out of their armchairs to put the kettle on.

Capricorns are domestic animals, and many of them live at home long after their contemporaries have flown the nest. Whilst other children are tearing round with their friends, the Capricorn prefers to stay with the adults.

Capricorns are very methodical people. Capricorn children can always find their toys, because each one has its place. When they come home from school, they put away their clothes neatly, have tea and then start their homework straight away. True Capricorns can't relax and enjoy life until they have done all their chores.

There is usually one person in the class who will play the fool and try to attract everyone's attention. But you will never find a Capricorn acting the clown. They just do not muck about. They are too serious for that.

Teachers enjoy having Capricorn pupils. They are industrious and pleasant. They do not spend their time daydreaming or messing up their work. They might not be so quick on the uptake, but it usually sinks in the end. It just takes them longer to learn things. And once they finally catch on, then they usually remember things forever.

As Capricorns tend to be loners, they sometimes find it hard to make friends. But usually the group ends up not only accepting them as they are, but liking them as well.

Good advice

Capricorns always want to plan everything down to the minutest detail. And whilst planning is a good thing, it is also wise to follow one's heart instead of one's mind now and again. Otherwise one can easily miss out on all the exciting things in life.

Earth and water compatibility

Water is necessary for all growth on earth, so people born under an earth sign usually get on well with those born under a water sign. One lot is down-to-earth and sensible, the other is more emotionally sensitive. And if they can avoid putting too much pressure on one another, then any cooperation will usually lead to a positive outcome.

But just as a plant can wither from overwatering, a relationship will founder if the Capricorn starts to feel that his or her Cancer or Virgo friend is being carried away by their emotions without due regard for the more down-to-earth Capricorn.

Capricorns get on better with Pisceans and Scorpions than with Cancerians.

Earth and air compatibility

These two signs are not very compatible. The practical,

cautious and down-to-earth Capricorn finds it hard to stomach the airy ideas which Geminis and Librans come up with. These will soon be dismissed by the Capricorn's common sense and eye for detail.

For their part, air sign people find Capricorns incredibly boring. And far too serious and never willing to have any fun.

They may be able to cooperate on the occasional project, where the Capricorn common sense can combine with the lively imagination of air sign people to good effect. But they do not make good partners in love.

Of all the air signs, Capricorns get on best with Aquarians.

Earth and fire compatibility

Fire sign people tend to bubble with life and the desire to do lots of exciting things. Capricorns never do anything unpremeditated or unplanned. So these two signs will often find it hard to get on. The Capricorns cannot understand how others can love new and exciting projects, especially when decisions have to be made quickly. They prefer things as they are, or at any rate to consider everything very carefully before making any changes.

But of course we don't want you to drop all your friends who don't belong to the right sign. For even though you may be very different, it doesn't necessarily mean that you are going to quarrel.

On the contrary, you can grow to understand those who think differently to you. And perhaps they can help you with things you are not so good at

Occupations

Subjects of Capricorn are fitted by their prudence, tact and extreme caution to be diplomats and negotiators of delicate business of all descriptions (Disraeli, Benjamin Franklin and Lord Curzon were all born under this sign). As officials, especially in the government, they are industrious and methodical, and usually rise to a position of authority. Other professions and trades which they may follow with profit are those of editor, actor, detective, architect, farmer, farrier, miner or mining official, metallurgist, dealer in lead or wool, and plumber.

Capricorns put a lot of effort into their work. They are not born leaders, but thanks to their hard work and single-mindedness, they often make it to the top anyway.

But they will not gain success at the expense of others. Capricorns will not push others aside in order to be first at the goal post. They prefer to make themselves indispensable.

Many Capricorns seek work in the educational field or in business. But there are also quite a few Capricorns in the art world.

Capricorns put so much into their work that they do not have much energy left for leisure activities. However, many of them enjoy music, either as performers or listeners.

Although they make very good back-room people, Capricornians can make good leaders and do well in their own businesses. Many have an affinity for scientific work and pay attention to detail. They work well with people, although they tend to have an isolationist attitude, taking advice only grudgingly. One might well find them in local government, finance, publishing, building or politics.

Health

Capricorn folk tend to be weak and ailing in childhood, though when they reach adult life they usually enjoy good health. The commonest ills of this type are injuries and diseases affecting the knees (which are ruled by Capricorn), as well as skin disorders, chills, rheumatism, constipation, toothache and earache. They should guard against anxiety and depression, for their complaints are often induced or aggravated by worry and introspection.

To attract good vibrations

The colours that will bring the most harmonious vibrations to Capricorn folk are black, grey and violet; all shades of the last two colours may be used.

Wider aspects

Those with Capricorn as their Sun sign are generally happy alone in leisure pursuits and therefore enjoy music, reading, etc.

Associations

Animals—dog and elephant.
Bird—owl.
Colour—dark colours.
Days—Saturday.
Flowers—pansy, ivy, nightshade and rue.
Food—starchy foods, meat.
Gemstones—amethyst, onyx for Capricorn; obsidian and jet for Saturn, its ruling planet.
Metal—lead.
Numbers—three for Capricorn; eight for Saturn.
Trees—pine, willow, cypress and yew.

Famous Capricorns

Dame Peggy Ashcroft	Actress
Humphrey Bogart	Actor
David Bowie	Singer, actor
Michael Crawford	Actor
Marlene Dietrich	Actress
Stefan Edberg	Tennis player

Kenny Everett	Comedian
Conrad Hilton	Hotelier
Anthony Hopkins	Actor
Nigel Kennedy	Violinist
Martin Luther King	Clergyman
Rudyard Kipling	Author
Annie Lennox	Singer
Henri Matisse	Painter
Sir Isaac Newton	Mathematician
Louis Pasteur	Bacteriologist
Elvis Presley	Singer
Dame Maggie Smith	Actress
J.R. Tolkien	Author
Mao Tse-tung	Communist leader

Aquarius

Dates

21 January to 18 February. The Sun enters the zodiacal sign Aquarius about January 21 and passes out of it on approximately February 18 each year, but since or about a week after its entry the influence of the previous sign, Capricorn, still remains in force, those born on the cusp—between January 21 and 27—are also ruled by Capricorn, and should consult the pages devoted to that sign as well.

Origin and glyph

There are several links with the water carrier, and the glyph clearly resembles water waves, although the similarity to serpents has also been noticed.

Ruling planet and groupings

Uranus; masculine, fixed and air.

Typical traits

Aquarians are renowned for their independence and the fact that they like to operate according to their own rules. This can lead to them becoming very stubborn, but they can be inspiring because they do not easily lose hope. Aquarians are friendly, although they may not be totally reliable when circumstances become difficult, and highly creative in terms of ideas. However, they are not necessarily sufficiently practical to see through the ideas. Overall, they may be a little perverse or paradoxical, but beneath it all is a gregariousness and a real wish to help.

Aquarius is the last of the airy signs. It is positive in magnetism, and is ruled by the mighty planets Saturn and Uranus; it is symbolized by a man holding a pitcher of water, which he or she pours upon the ground.

Persons born under Aquarius are generally idealistic, generous and humane, and are quick to relieve the distress or wants of others. They are very shrewd judges of human nature, and are acutely sensitive to outside impressions, with a natural gift for immediately sensing the magnetic auras of any persons or places with which they come into contact.

Seeking eternally after truth and beauty, they are strong champions of progress in every direction, longing to sweep away all that is corrupt and burdensome, even though it may have become sanctified by age and long custom, and to replace it with something more serviceable to the needs and welfare of humanity. Three leading examples of this type are Abraham Lincoln, Charles Dickens, and Philip Mclancthon, the reformer.

Though gifted with great insight and intuition, their reasoning powers are also active, and they do not depend upon feeling alone for their impressions or opinions, but must debate everything in their own mind in a logical fashion. When once they have formed their conclusions, however, their opinions are unalterable.

Aquarians are cheerful and reliable friends and are usually very popular, since they have social gifts of a high order. They deeply appreciate the affection of others, and respond eagerly to the least show of friendship; but at the same time, their feelings are easily affronted, and slights and injuries which would leave many people unaffected are nursed and brooded over for a long time.

Aquarians are usually strong intellectually, and though they are eager to welcome fresh and novel ideas, they refuse to take anything on trust, but insist on its being demonstrated fully and satisfactorily before they will accept it. They are keenly attracted by science especially by electricity and magnetism—and by any invention or new line of thought that promises to increase the happiness of humanity. Among leading scientists, thinkers, and others who have helped the human race, Francis Bacon, Swedenborg, Copernicus,

Charles Darwin, Ernst Haeckel, Sir Hiram Maxim and Thomas Alva Edison were all born under the sign of Aquarius.

The dual rulership of this sign—by both Saturn and Uranus makes its natives contradictory in many ways. Under the influence of Saturn, they may be cautious, indolent, restrained in their passions, and rather slow-going and dull. But at other times, under the sway of Uranus, the same people may surprise their friends by an entire alteration of character for a time, when they defy convention, break old ties and habits, and probably display eccentricity or strange flashes of genius.

Aquarians often have fine talents or incipient genius lying latent and undeveloped in their subconsciousness, and unfortunately it may be on rare occasions only that these are ever called to the surface—usually in emergencies and at the urge of necessity. Many such people, apparently quite ordinary and undistinguished, might rise to a high place in the world if they would but apply themselves to developing these hidden powers.

Not surprisingly, Aquarians like the freedom to do whatever they want, and they tend not to heed anyone who tries to boss them around. They are highly inventive and are generally good with any subject of a technical nature. They are also highly competent at practicalities. This makes for a considerable range of occupations, and Aquarians often turn their hand to science, communications, teaching, social work and general administration.

Have you ever come across a girl who turns up at parties in her grandmother's old dresses? Or a boy who likes to flaunt new and quite outrageous hairstyles? If you have, then they are bound to be Aquarians.

But you should also realise that that crazy hairstyle or that weird notion of wearing granny's old clothes may become the fashion in a couple of years. For Aquarians have a knack of being ahead of their time. One could even say that they live in the future.

Aquarians hate anything ordinary and detest doing the same as everyone else. They love to shock people and to create scandals.

Aquarians are unpredictable. You can never be certain of how an Aquarian is going to react. If an Aquarian girl decides to knit a sweater, she won't bother to use a pattern. And even if she does, she is bound to try to 'improve' on the original idea. Nor will she have much use for a cookery book, preferring to create a new dish by trying various combinations of her own creation.

Aquarians are sometimes regarded as slightly eccentric by other people. But it is a fact that more geniuses have been born under the sign of Aquarius than under any of the other signs.

Inferior or undeveloped subjects of Aquarius may be indolent, timid, neurotic, revengeful, dishonest, unscrupulous and false to their word. In financial matters Aquarians are usually fortunate, but, whether they be rich or poor, money is often a worry or a source of misfortune to them.

Aquarians are happy and successful in any kind of scientific research, but especially in connection with electricity. This sign also produces talented musicians, actors, and poets, such as Mozart, Schubert, Mendelssohn, David Garrick, Sir Henry Irving, Joseph Jefferson, Lord Byron and Robert Burns were also born under Aquarius.

This sign particularly favours the callings of psychologist, company promoter, aviator, electrician, ship's carpenter and nurse or keeper of the insane.

Relationships and love

Aquarius folk are romantic and idealistic, and are apt to set the object of their affections upon a pedestal, so that they are bitterly disappointed and grieved when their beloved's human frailties become apparent. The consequent disillusionment gives rise to much unhappiness, until the partners become adjusted to one another by the process of time. Usually Aquarians are faithful and loyal in matrimony, but they may be quite the opposite. At the best of times their sudden moods and caprices are liable to cause perplexity and pain to friends and marriage partner alike.

Good friends are often born under the same sign or at any rate belong to the same element. Aquarius is an air sign which means that Aquarians get on well with the other air signs, Libra and Gemini.

Aquarians need a lot of security, which they try to reinforce by surrounding themselves with other people. A true Aquarian will often have a lot of friends, but will not necessarily form emotional attachments to many of them.

If you ask an Aquarian friend for a word of advice or his opinion, you will get a straightforward, honest answer. But if this upsets you he or she will not shed a tear with you in sympathy. Nor will he or she try to change you. An Aquarian thinks that that is your problem and your responsibility, and would not want anyone to try to run his life for him.

If you make friends with an Aquarian, you will find him a very loyal person. He will not be moved by gossip. He might listen to your enemies having a bitch about you out of sheer curiosity. But you can safely assume that he will rely on his own judgement rather than others.

Because of their independence, Aquarians may find it difficult to establish an emotional tie. However, providing they find the right type, who is not weak but capable and sensible, personal relationships can be very successful. They are usually totally faithful.

Aquarians are not great romantics, who dream of the great love of their life. If you fall for an Aquarian, your chances will be greater if you are also best friends. And should you by any chance be planning on spending the rest of your life on a desert island together with the Aquarian of your dreams, you will probably find yourself rowing out there on your own.

Aquarians cherish their independence, so there is no point in fooling yourself that you can have one all to yourself. On the other hand, Aquarians are happy to let you have your own friends and interests without interfering. They are not at all inclined to jealousy .

Aquarians find it quite hard to express their emotions. For instance, if you haven't seen your partner for a long time and are expecting a great love scene when you are reunited again, then you will certainly be disappointed. The old cliché 'out of sight, out of mind' fits the Aquarian like a glove. Your partner may well seem quite cold, even though he or she really does like you.

If you want to hold on to your Aquarian then you mustn't be jealous or possessive. Never say: 'You can't do that—what would other people think?', if you do, you can start looking for someone else straight away.

With children, they are supportive but may find it diffi-cult to cope with emotional problems.

They should mate, if possible, with those born between May 21 and June 21 and between September 21 and Octo-ber 21.

Children

Aquarians become socially adept at a very early age. Whereas other children will start quarrelling over a toy, a four year-old Aquarian will probably suggest sharing in-stead. And the Aquarian child is quite happy to take his or her favourite toy along when he or she goes to play with other children. The only trouble is that the child will often forget to bring it home again.

Children may be a little unconventional, and some school environments may not be conducive to the full development of their potential. On the positive side, children will be originators, naturally friendly, and show the Aquarian traits of creativity and an affinity for science. The natural friendliness should not, however, be allowed to develop into a trust of anyone, particularly strangers.

Aquarians can be quite stubborn. They are always convinced that their ideas are best. Nonetheless they prefer to work in groups because they love being with other people. These two characteristics are not very compatible and can cause a lot of problems for them.

Aquarians are almost insatiably curious. They love solving mysteries and they do not give up until they have found out how things work.

If the teacher is reading the story of Snow White to the class, the true Aquarian will probably be more interested in the nature of the poison the wicked stepmother used to try and kill Snow White than whether she recovers or not.

Provided it is harnessed properly, the Aquarian curiosity will produce good marks for its owner. But very often the school report will contain remarks about the Aquarian tendency to daydream instead of concentrating in class. And since they were not exactly at the front of the queue when good memories were being dished out, they have a tendency to forget their homework, which is thus not always due to laziness.

Aquarian people want to choose what they do themselves—and that goes for schoolwork too. They get round the exercises set by the teacher either by picking the easiest problems or by simply claiming that they can't do them.

Good advice

Aquarians like working with other people, but still think they should be the boss. It wouldn't be a bad idea for Aquarians to try listening to what others have to say instead of thinking that they are the only ones who are right.

Nor is it always such a bright idea to go for every new thing that turns up, believing that everything new is automatically good and everything old useless.

Occupations

Aquarians are often frustrated when trying to reconcile their childhood dreams of performing great deeds or their ambitions of achieving great fame with the real world. The boys dream of becoming deep sea divers and astronauts, and the girls long to become great politicians or the Prima Ballerina. This does not make it easy to settle for a job as a clerk or till lady.

The Aquarian has lots of different interests, but tires of them very easily. He or she is always interested in the latest ideas and fads, and loves science fiction books and movies.

Ideal jobs for Aquarians are those which deal with people like teaching. But they prefer unusual careers such as inventor, research worker or writer.

Not surprisingly, Aquarians like the freedom to do whatever they want, and tend not to heed anyone who tries to boss them around. They are highly inventive and are generally good with any subject of a technical nature. They are also highly competent at practicalities. This makes for a considerable range of occupations, and Aquarians of ten turn their hand to science, communications teaching, social work and general administration.

Air and earth compatibility

Those born under an air sign or an earth sign often find it difficult to understand each other. The first group have all sorts of pie-in-the-sky plans and ideas, and can't comprehend why the more down-to-earth Taureans or Capricorns don't fall for these ideas straight away, but tend to be regular wet blankets.

But just as the plants and animals of the earth benefit

from the oxygen in the air, air and earth sign people can profit from one another. But they are heading for trouble as soon as one tries to dominate the other.

Of all the earth signs, Aquarians get on best with Virgos.

Air and fire compatibility

Air signs are often somewhat frivolous, and fire signs barge ahead, not always allowing for thought before action. These two signs get on well with one another, because an Aquarius person would never dream of stopping an Aries or a Sagittarius person in mid flight. On the contrary, they are more likely to encourage any project or even join in, regardless of how daring it may be.

People born under these two signs do not seem to be bothered by the fact that they are somewhat detached from reality. But it does look as though they are destined to be best friends rather than partners.

Aquarians get on better with Arians and Sagittarians than with Leos.

Air and water compatibility

Air and water signs can learn a lot from each other. Whereas Aquarians are usually very self-confident, a water sign such as a Pisces person may often doubt his own worth. On the other hand the Aquarian person has trouble expressing his emotions, and can receive a lot of help in this respect from the more sensitive water signs.

It is a well-known fact that you cannot breathe under water, and this image is transferable to the water and air signs. They can have a suffocating effect on each other, if one of them tries to dominate.

Of all the water signs, Aquarians get on best with Cancerians.

But of course we don't want you to drop all your friends

who don't belong to the right sign. For even though you may be very different, it doesn't necessarily mean that you are going to quarrel.

On the contrary, you can grow to understand those who think differently to you. And perhaps they can help you with things you are not so good at.

Health

Aquarius rules the legs and ankles, and these members are more prone to injury—by sprains, fractures and the like—than any other part of the body. The circulation of the blood also comes under this sign, and may be liable to disorder. Uranus gives a tendency to electric shocks and danger from lightning. Aquarians are often keenly interested in hygiene, food reform, dietetics and similar subjects, and by practising these things are often able to keep themselves in splendid health.

To attract good vibrations

Electric blue and electric green are the most harmonious colours for Aquarius, and if worn on the person and freely used in other ways they will be found to act as receivers of beneficial astral vibrations.

Wider aspects

Aquarians are by their very nature a little out on a limb and unconventional, but their very positive qualities make this an interesting Sun sign.

Associations

Animal—dog.
Bird—cuckoo.
Colour—electric blue.

Day—Saturday.

Gemstones—aquamarine, zircon and garnet for Aquarius; malachite, ruby, jet and black onyx for Saturn; jacinth and jargoon for Uranus.

Number—two.

Flowers—orchid, snowdrop and foxglove.

Food—a light diet is best, including fruits.

Metal—platinum.

Trees—pine, fruit trees.

Famous Aquarians

Lord Byron	Poet
Phil Collins	Musician, actor
Charles Darwin	Naturalist
James Dean	Actor
Charles Dickens	Author
Christian Dior	Fashion designer
Placido Domingo	Opera singer
Mia Farrow	Actress
Benny Hill	Comedian
James Joyce	Author
Norman Mailer	Author
John McEnroe	Tennis player
Wolfgang A. Mozart	Composer
Paul Newman	Actor
Vanessa Redgrave	Actress
Telly Savalas	Actor
Jules Verne	Author
Virginia Woolf	Author

Pisces

Dates

19 February to 20 March. The Sun enters Pisces about February 19 and leaves this sign about March 20. Persons born between February 19 and 27 are also partly ruled by the preceding sign, Aquarius, and they should, therefore, study the characteristics given by this sign as well.

Origin and glyph

There are numerous links between the two fishes and various deities from history, including Jesus Christ. The glyph represents two fish, linked, but also refers to the physical and spiritual side of the person.

Ruling planet and groupings

Neptune; feminine, mutable and water.

Typical traits

It is not easy to recognise somebody born under the sign of Pisces, for all the other eleven signs are combined in this one. In other words, sometimes a Piscean will behave like a Leo, and at other times like an Aries or a Gemini.

But traits which are common to most Pisceans are sensitivity and a caring nature. Pisceans are impressionable people and they are quick to express sympathy for others.

In March the weather can shift dramatically from warm and sunny to snow, frost, rain or fog. The Piscean's moods vary in the same way. Pisceans will shed floods of tears when they feel hurt, and can sink into such a mire of self-pity, that they are a pain to be with. But fortunately, just as the sun soon breaks through again, so too the Piscean's mood will brighten up.

Pisces people need lots of praise if they are to make a success of things. But where a Leo or an Aries will swallow it lock, stock and barrel, a Piscean will know whether your praise is sincere and deserved.

The Piscean person is really quite sensitive but above all is a highly sympathetic and caring person who invariably puts other people first, especially the family. They have great intuition and are good at understanding the needs of other people and make very good, kind friends. Sometimes they can take their idealistic and self-effacing stance too far, resulting in an unwillingness to face decisions, and sometimes they will rely on other, stronger, characters to lead for them. They are usually always tactful but should beware that helping others and becoming involved emotionally is not always a good thing.

Pisces is a watery and negative sign, and is ruled by the two planets Jupiter and Neptune. Its symbol is two fishes, attached yet turning in opposite directions, which typify the dual nature of those born under this sign, who often intend one thing and do another. Gifted with wide vision and a rich imagination, they are capable of conceiving lofty and grandiose schemes; but when they are called on to put them into action, grow timid and lose confidence.

Natives of Pisces are exceedingly romantic, kind-hearted and emotional, but are so lacking in stability and willpower, and are so sensitive to rebuffs and discouragement, that the amount of good which they achieve falls far short of their intentions. They are retiring, vacillating and sadly lacking in ambition, and yet, if constantly urged forward with encouragement and sympathy, they may easily climb the heights of fame and success, for they are often talented, are very apt at learning and accumulating knowledge, and possess a quiet sort of persistence which is peculiar to them.

Pisces subjects readily absorb impressions and take on the psychic auras of people with whom they are brought into contact, and thus their judgment is often clouded and their opinions are unreliable. For this reason, when they are obliged to make an important decision, they should ponder the matter carefully when alone and act resolutely upon their own intuition, without allowing it to be vitiated by the influence of others.

Pisces subjects are fond of comfort and a quiet life, and they will invariably take the easiest path that offers itself. But the superior Pisces folk—and even many of the weaker types—are capable of making the most signal sacrifices when necessity demands, and will then endure an extraordinary amount of suffering and privation without complaint.

A love of order and social convention characterizes those born under this sign, yet they are always ready to find an excuse for the transgressions of others; for, not having much real vice themselves, they simply cannot recognize it in the people around them.

Natives of Pisces are usually fond of animals and children and may have considerable influence over them, ruling them by kindness rather than severity. They may become powerfully attracted towards the study of the occult, and, if very weak, may be completely ruled by superstition. Their telepathic and intuitive powers are often highly developed, and they make good mediums, thought-readers and psychic investigators.

Many of the finest and most enlightened types of mankind are born under Pisces, and many of its natives achieve renown, high rank, honours and riches. But the great majority of those born under this sign are burdened with such a heavy inferiority complex that they stand constantly in need of a stimulus to bring them up to the mark.

Relationships and love
They like to be petted and fussed over, and are often very attractive to the opposite sex. But their vows, promises and affectionate ways are not to be relied on, and a measure of

firmness on the part of their partner in marriage is usually desirable.

Good friends are often born under the same sign or at any rate belong to the same element. Pisces is a water sign, so this means that Pisceans get on well with the other water signs, Scorpio and Cancer.

If you need a shoulder to cry on, then it is handy to have a Pisces person as a friend. But you may find that the Piscean gets so caught up in your problems that he or she ends up crying twice as much as you. On the other hand you won't be criticised for whatever you have done. The Pisces person is very understanding and will not be shocked nor disappointed in you.

Pisceans often stand up for the weakest group, which also means that they are sometimes exploited because they find it hard to say no to others.

Pisceans cannot cope with disappointments, which anyhow they find difficult to avoid as they are so concerned with the welfare of others. Many Pisceans tend to console themselves with food. This is a vicious circle: they feel sorry for themselves because they are too fat, and so they need consolation, and eat even more.

In partnerships, Pisceans can be a little difficult to cope with, but with the right partner they will build a welcoming home. They like visitors and to visit others and their self-sacrificing attitude means that they will usually go a little further to make people happy, or an occasion just right. It is important that their lack of strong will is not exploited by a stronger character.

Pisces people are highly emotional and when a Piscean really takes a fancy to someone he or she will fall head over heels in love. But here too they find it hard to distinguish between fantasy and reality, and a Pisces girl will thus experience terrible disappointment when her knight on a white charger turns out to be just an ordinary guy on a rusty old bike. Pisces people want to believe in the best in others so much that they fit the old adage 'love is blind' better than anyone else.

If a Pisces' sweetheart does not live up to expectations, then the Piscean can always withdraw into a world of day-dreams, just as he or she did as a child with no friends.

If you are going out with a Piscean then you cannot afford to have a jealous nature, because the Piscean tendency to listen and be sympathetic to others draws people to him or her. But do not let this confuse you, for Pisces people are faithful by nature. In return, you are expected to be just as loyal and reliable. Once you have understood this, you will find there is no more loving a sweetheart than a Pisces.

If you have a Pisces girlfriend you will find that she does not try to dominate or to change you. She will accept you as you are.

Pisceans love children and make very good parents providing they are not too soft. They do have an inner strength, and can be very tough and resourceful if the occasion demands it and when they rise to the challenge. Children often take second place to others and may need some help with their self-confidence. However, they can be very good in science and with parental encouragement can be good achievers.

Subjects of Pisces are most deeply in harmony with people born between June 21 and July 21 and between October 21 and November 21. They are full of sentiment, and their sympathy is easily excited.

Children

Pisceans need to fulfil a strong feeling of belonging. If they have no friends or playmates, then they will often invent one. And with their vivid imagination, the imaginary friend can be almost as real as one made of flesh and blood.

If an Aries child can't get its own way, it becomes so cross and stroppy that parents will usually give in for the sake of peace.

Pisces children are not like that at all. Instead, the Pisces child will smother its parents in sweet talk and smiles, and in no time at all will charm its parents into giving in.

Pisceans find school very difficult, because they hate time-tables and regulations. And they find it hard to adapt to any routine which they have not dictated themselves. On the other hand, their creativity and imagination can help them to solve difficult tasks in a highly untraditional way.

Pisceans are not usually very academic, but they excel in the creative subjects such as music and art.

Pisceans are susceptible to teasing, and if they feel victim-ised they will withdraw into their own world, where they sometimes find it difficult to distinguish between fantasy and reality. This also means that Pisceans will find them-selves been scolded for elaborating on the truth, even though this is not done on purpose to deceive.

Pisces people understand people well and never condemn others outright. If for instance you tell a Piscean that you have been quarrelling with your brother as you had to 'bor-row' his bike in order to get to the station on time, he or she would not dream of saying that was a cheek, or that it was quite natural for your brother to be cross. No, your Pisces friend will politely ask whether you got there on time, or whether the film you went to see was any good.

Good advice
Pisceans are easily influenced, because they are so uncer-tain of themselves. The best advice one can give a Piscean is to stick by his or her own feelings and opinions.

Water and air compatibility
Air signs like Libra and Aquarius can learn a lot from the

water signs, and vice versa. Pisces people for instance, find it hard to understand that other people are different to themselves and think in different ways. The air signs are much better at this. On the other hand the water signs can teach the air signs to understand their own emotions.

Water and the air signs can get on well with each other, although some air sign people find it hard to take the highly strung and emotionally unstable Pisceans.

Air can create high seas and wild storms. Similar things happen when an Aquarian or a Gemini shows too little consideration for the oversensitive Piscean. Then the Piscean atmospheric barometer plunges below zero!

Pisceans seem to get on best with Librans.

Water and earth compatibility

Water is essential for all growth on the earth. So people born under an earth sign usually get on well with Pisceans. One is down-to-earth, the other more emotional. So if they do not try to dominate each other but respect each other's idiosyncrasies, they can derive a lot of pleasure from each other's company.

But just as a plant will die from overwatering, a friendship can be destroyed if the Piscean gets wrapped up in his own emotions to the exclusion of the more materialistic concerns of Taurus, Virgo or Capricorn people.

Of all the earth signs, Pisces people get on best with Capricornians and Taureans.

Water and fire compatibility

These two elements are normally not very compatible. As we know, water extinguishes fire. A Pisces person simply cannot understand an Arian or a Taurean who comes dashing in with some half-baked project to be carried out right away.

On the other hand, people born under a fire sign get very frustrated by Pisceans who always seem so passive and have to take so many things into consideration before making any decision.

Occupations

Travel, especially on the water, seems to exert a great fascination for Pisces folk, and this, coupled with their characteristic love of delving into the mysterious and unknown, may produce a genius for exploration; notable examples are David Livingstone and Arminius Vambéry. Pisces subjects may also have a strong gift for music, literature and philosophy, occupations in which their intense imagination can have full play, and this sign has produced such great artists and thinkers as Chopin, Handel, Rossini, Michelangelo, Ibsen, Victor Hugo, Longfellow, Montaigne, Cardinal Newman, Ernest Renan, Schopenhauer and Ellen Terry.

It is not surprising, with their caring instincts, that Pisceans make good teachers and members of the health and related professions. They tend not to be particularly ambitious but can have extremely good business minds. Success is usually more likely if they have a supportive business partner. Other professions that often attract Pisceans include acting, the ministry, and anything linked with the sea.

A Pisces person usually chooses a career which involves working with people, like a nurse or a doctor. Zone therapy and healing are also obvious choices, as the Piscean is strongly attracted by mysticism. Many Pisceans develop their creative talents and become artists, actors or musicians.

Pisceans also spend their leisure time on creative activities. They enjoy listening to music, or going to the theatre. And they like water, both for drinking, or swimming.

Among the more prosaic occupations favoured by this sign are those of commercial traveller, sailor, brewer, fishmonger, teacher, nurse, leather-worker and dealer in boots and shoes; also any occupation connected with children and animals.

Health

Pisces rules the feet and toes, and these parts are particularly liable to disease and injury. Among the most common ailments affecting subjects of Pisces are chills, gout, dropsy, sluggishness of the liver and infectious diseases. They should guard also against disorders arising from the pleasures of the table, of which they are usually very fond.

To attract good vibrations

The most magnetic colours for Pisces folk are purple, mauve, and sea-green; these should be freely used in clothing and in household decorations.

Wider aspects

Pisceans have to be careful that in helping and caring for others they tend to ignore their own pursuits or problems.

Associations

Animals—sheep and ox.
Birds—swan and stork.
Colour—sea green.
Day—Thursday.
Flowers—heliotrope, water lily and carnation.
Food—excesses should be avoided, salad foods are suitable.
Gemstones—moonstone, sapphire and emerald for Pisces; amethyst for Jupiter, and coral for Neptune, its rulers.
Metal—tin.
Numbers—six for Pisces; three for both Jupiter and Neptune.
Trees—willow and elm.

Famous Pisceans

Edward Albee	Playwright
Harry Belafonte	Actor, singer
Michael Caine	Actor
Jasper Carrott	Comedian
Frederic Chopin	Composer
Nat King Cole	Singer, pianist
Albert Einstein	Physicist
Victor Hugo	Novelist, poet
David Livingstone	Explorer
Michelangelo	Sculptor, painter
Liza Minnelli	Actress
David Niven	Actor
Rudolf Nureyev	Ballet dancer
Anita Roddick	Businesswoman, founder of the Body Shop
Elizabeth Taylor	Actress
Antonio Vivaldi	Composer

Your Birth Chart

Constructing a Chart

All the foregoing is background information that helps in the interpretation of a birth chart or horoscope. A typical blank chart is shown on page 189. The solid central line represents the horizon and the numbered segments are the houses, as described previously. On this chart are plotted the positions of the Sun, Moon and planets.

To begin with, the following information about the subject is required:

—the date of birth,

—the time of birth and whether it was British Summer Time or not, and

—the place of birth and the appropriate latitude and longitude.

From the information, the position of the ascendant and midheaven can be plotted, followed by the planets' positions. As each planet is placed on the chart there will be certain angular positions developed between them, and when these form specific angles they are called *aspects*. These aspects have considerable influence on the chart and therefore on its subject.

In addition to these factors, there are further interpretive factors depending on the placing of the planets in the various signs and the positions of that same planet in one of the twelve houses.

All these different parts of astrology are considered in further detail next.

Astrological aspects

The word 'aspects' has a particularly significant meaning in astrology. These are the angular relationships that plan-

Constructing aspects

ets make with each other and also with the ascendant, midheaven, descendant and nadir. On a birth chart the aspects appear as lines joining the planets to each other, and often these are also displayed in a grid, using another set of glyphs in a kind of shorthand notation.

Aspects form a qualifying statement about the planets and, depending on their effect, can be called easy or difficult, or, alternatively, the degree of their effect may be classed as positive, negative or weak. Hence, some aspects will make life easier for the subjects while others will introduce difficulties. Other factors should also be taken into account, namely the nature of the planets concerned and the houses and signs in which they occur.

An aspect is considered valid only if the respective planets are within a certain number of degrees of each other. The width or range allowed is called the *orb*, and, not surprisingly, an exact aspect is much stronger than a wide one. There is some difference in the size of the orbs used by different astrologers, but major aspects commonly have an orb of 8 degrees while others are 4 degrees, and for those aspects with only a minor influence, the orb may be 2 degrees.

The different aspects with appropriate glyphs are listed below, starting with the *major aspects*:

Major aspects

Conjunction
Conjunction ☌ can be positive or negative. A conjunction is when two planets or a planet and the ascendant are located close to each other (within the 8 degrees orb). If the planets fall in the same sign then the aspect is strengthened. Conversely, it is weakened if one falls into an adjacent sign, although it does depend upon the planet. The conjunction is the most powerful of all aspects and confers a strong personality.

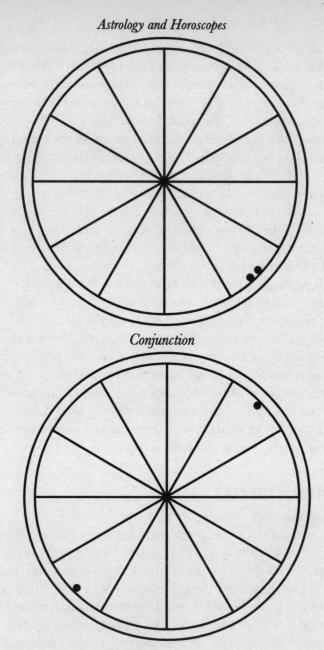

Conjunction

Opposition

Constructing a Chart

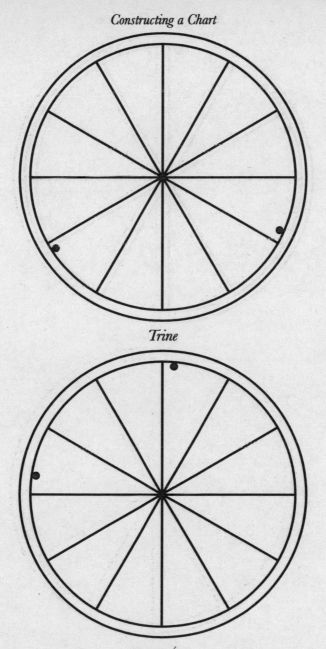

Trine

Square

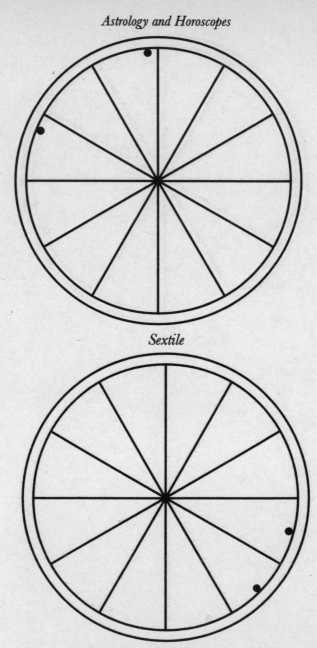

Sextile

Semi-sextile

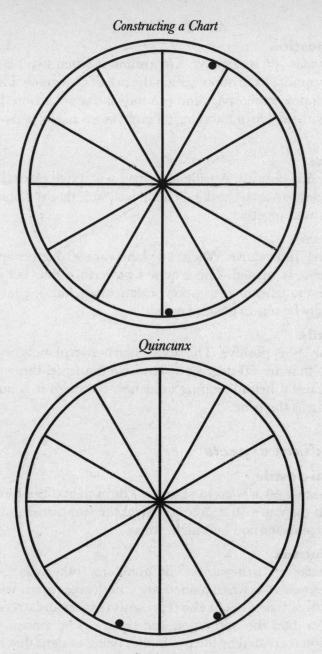

Constructing a Chart

Quincunx

Semi-square

Oppostion

Opposition ☍ is negative. Opposition is when two planets are opposite each other, within the orb of 8 degrees. This is also a powerful aspect and can indicate problems in dealing with people or handling different facets of the personality.

Trine

Trine △ is positive. A trine is formed when two planets are 120 degrees apart and in general indicates that the planets work well together.

Square

Square☐ is negative. When two planets are 90 degrees apart, a square is formed. This is quite a powerful aspect but may represent tension, disruption or difficulties, although it can equally be put to positive ends.

Sextile

Sextile ⚹ is positive. The sextile marks two planets or features that are 60 degrees apart. Like the trine, the sextile indicates a helpful, easing influence, although it is not as strong as the trine.

Medium aspects

Semi-sextile

Semi-sextile ⚺ is weak to negative. The semi-sextile is formed when there are 30 degrees between the two planets, and it represents tension and slight stress.

Quincunx

Quincunx ⚻ is negative. The quincunx (otherwise called the *inconjunct*) is when planets are 150 degrees apart within an orb of 2 degrees. It also represents tension and stress but less so than the opposition and square. The tendency to tension is created by the two bodies being in signs that have no relationship with each other through triplicity,

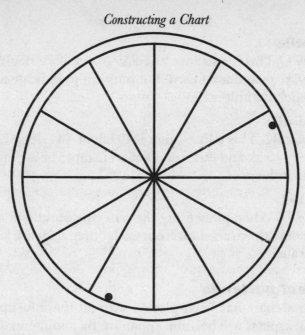

Sesquiquadrate

quadruplicity, etc. It can be very difficult to live with.

Minor aspects

Semi-square

Semi-square ∠ is negative. If the angular separation between planets is 45 degrees, a semi-square is formed. Since
it has some connection with the square, it generally represents difficulties.

Sesquiquadrate

Sesquiquadrate ⬡ is weak to negative. The sesquiquadrate,
or *sesquare*, is when an angle of 135 degrees separates the
planets. Again it has obvious connections to the square and
accordingly represents difficulties.

Quintile

Quintile Q This is a strange angular aspect of 72 degrees. It is very weak and little used, but is meant to indicate a generally helpful influence.

Biquintile

Biquintile BC This is like Quintile Q but of 144 degrees. It is also very weak and little used but is meant to be a generally helpful influence.

Parallel

Parallel | | When planets are the same measurement above and below the ascendant from each other, they are said to be parallel.

Aspect patterns

When a chart has been plotted with all the information, certain aspects will become apparent. By joining up the information in a particular construction, certain patterns are formed that have influence upon the subject's personality, and they can work to his or her benefit or detriment.

Upon establishing a particular aspect, a point is made midway between the centre of the chart and the planet on the periphery. Lines then join these points for each aspect, creating a chart with several geometric shapes that are discussed below. It is often the case that different aspects are drawn with different lines (solid, dotted, dashed, etc) or several colours are used to help differentiate between oppositions, trines, sextiles, and so on.

There are a number of *aspect patterns*, which may involve three or four planets. It is generally the case that all the planets form aspects. If, however, there is an unaspected planet it will be a very powerful feature but may represent personality problems. The main aspect patterns are:

Tee-square

This configuration consists of two planets in opposition with

Constructing a Chart

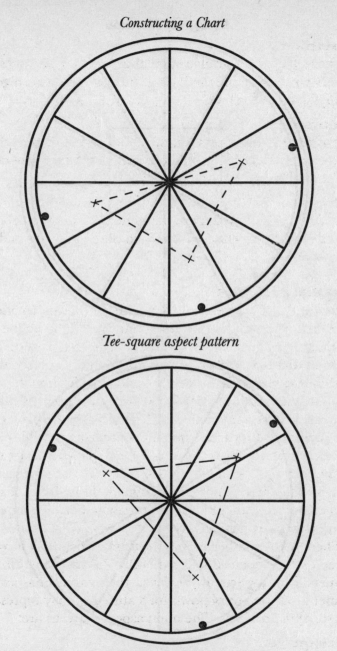

Tee-square aspect pattern

Grand trine aspect pattern

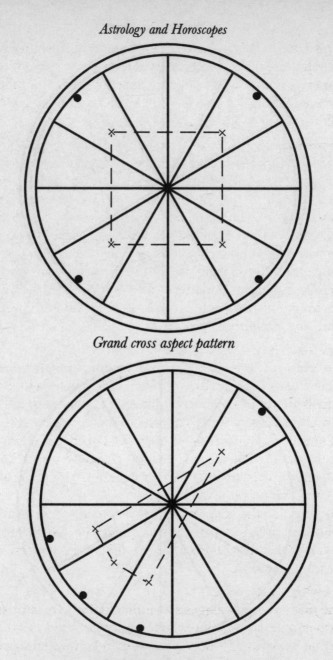

Grand cross aspect pattern

The pointer aspect pattern

a third that makes a square aspect to both of the other planets. All the aspects so constructed are negative, but it often confers strength. A great deal depends upon the planets involved, but it can be a forceful, dynamic subject with this pattern.

Grand trine

The grand trine is a triangular aspect formation with three trine aspects. At first sight this is a positive aspect, but it does depend greatly on other factors. For example, there may be a tendency to laziness and weakness of character, and if more than three planets make up the trine, there is the tendency for the element that is highlighted to become too strong. Charts should be studied carefully, however, as there are often other patterns that compensate. For example, the presence of a tee-square pattern will add some solidity and strength to the character.

Grand cross

The grand cross is not a common feature, but when it does occur it forms a very strong influence. It is made up of four planets in a four-cornered square such that there are two oppositions comprising planets at opposite corners. In addition, the four planets make square aspects with their adjacent planet. The result is that it is a very powerful feature and can be disruptive, although its effect may be lessened by other aspect patterns.

Because of the separation of the four planets, each will fall in the same quadruplicity or quality, i.e. fixed, mutable or cardinal. This confers a slightly different perspective on the interpretation.

Fixed grand cross

The *fixed grand cross* suggests an individual who may be stubborn or at least someone who tolerates the *status quo*. It may be that he or she has been put upon and criticized so much that he or she has given up.

Mutable grand cross

The *mutable grand cross* implies adaptability and potentially an ability to overcome obstacles and work around problems. There may still be nervous stress because although the subject will opt for an easy solution and a straightforward life, other factors may prohibit this, such as a feeling of duty.

Cardinal grand cross

The *cardinal grand cross* essentially implies a desire and a will to overcome difficulties. A lack of self-confidence may prove a barrier, but, with sufficient determination, this can be overcome and result in considerable achievement.

Pointer

A pointer aspect pattern is made up of two planets in opposition and one of these two then forms quincunx aspects with two further planets, producing a pattern shaped like an arrowhead.

The quincunx and opposition are both indicative of tension and stress, and this is compounded by two semi-sextile patterns at the other end of the pointer. Overall, then, this is a stressful pattern, and in many cases it focuses, at its point, on the house of importance.

Stellium

A final pattern that may occur is when three or more planets occur in one house or sign, and this implies a reinforcing of the concerns of the house or the characteristics of the sign. This arrangement is called a *stellium*, and can cause a certain imbalance in a subject's chart because of the emphasis it applies. The extreme qualities of the sign involved may be accentuated, and it helps to look to other planets to counterbalance this effect.

Aspects of the Planets

In this section each planet is considered in relation to the others by way of the aspects formed. In each case the conjunction and then positive and negative aspects are described with regard to how they affect the overall picture. Reference can be made to the preceding list of aspects and whether they are positive or negative.

The Sun

Aspects made by the Sun to other planets are very important in interpreting charts, and planets aspected to the Sun will be strengthened. The effect of the planet or planets on the Sun shows how its own influence will be manifested. If the Sun aspects with the ruling planet of the chart then it is very important.

Sun/Moon aspects

In conjunction these planets generally confer harmony, and there is an emphasis on characteristics associated with the sign. The conjunction may not always be in the same sign or house. If this happens, it may reflect an inner conflict normally associated with negative aspects. Positive aspects between the Sun and Moon represent a coherence and oneness of the personality, while negative aspects mirror the likelihood of unsatisfied restlessness. Minor aspects will have little influence and will have a subsidiary role in the presence of other features.

Sun/Mercury aspects

Because the Sun and Mercury are never more than 28 degrees apart, the only aspects that can occur are a conjunction or semi-sextile. If the conjunction is close, less than 5 degrees, it is customarily taken that the subject will be a slow developer, although experience does not necessarily confirm this. In general these aspects confer an energetic and positive outlook. If the planets are in the same sign, the subject will think and express himself or herself in the nature of that sign.

Sun/Venus aspects

The Sun and Venus are never more than 48 degrees apart, so the only aspects possible are a conjunction, semi-sextile and semi-square. A conjunction represents affection, and the individual will probably enjoy the pleasurable aspects of life, often to excess. Other characteristics that may be strengthened or emerge are kindness and gentility, but, to excess, the overall result can be laziness and a certain irresponsibility. The semi-sextile will never be a strong feature, but it does indicate creativity and an appreciation of finer things, for example, art or music. If the semi-square occurs, it can indicate a rift in personal relationships.

Sun/Mars aspects

If the Sun and Mars occur in conjunction, there is a very strong positive, and cumulative, effect. Because of the individual effects of these planets, Mars for physical energy and the Sun for vitality, this conjunction is particularly forceful. This may also apply to the emotional picture of the individual. The bold, brave traits may be taken to the point of heroism but may equally result in overwork. Positive aspects have much the same effect but with a beneficial outcome and without treading on anyone's toes. Negative aspects include angry outbursts but more commonly the bad effects of overwork.

Sun/Jupiter aspects

In many ways a conjunction of the Sun with Jupiter can be regarded as highly fortuitous. It represents a general contentment, but more, people with this conjunction are held to be very 'lucky' as they will probably have considerable good fortune and opportunities in life. There tends to be a feeling that good luck can be expected. The outward-looking and expansive nature associated with Jupiter can result in an ambitious, intelligent and humorous individual. Positive aspects will have much the same result, and although the individual may not be particularly competitive strength may be seen in certain sports.

Negative aspects may include conceit, impudence and extravagance and a tendency to exaggerate, although these may be lessened to some extent if there are other, steadying influences in the chart.

Sun/Saturn aspects

It has been understood for some time that Saturn has a dampening effect on the Sun, cancelling out to some extent its vitality. Thus, in conjunction, Saturn will cause the Sun's effect to be limited and the cumulative result will depend very much on other planetary aspects. If other aspects are mainly positive then the effect of Saturn will be limited. Positive aspects introduce patience and a practical outlook on life, and although there may be shyness, it can be overcome.

The negative aspects are often manifested in a lack of self-confidence, and this may result, with other factors, in a tendency to ill health.

Sun/Uranus aspects

The Sun in conjunction with Uranus can be extremely strong and result in someone who is rebellious or rather eccentric. It may, however, also confer originality and independence, and there is often a scientific ability. Positive aspects can have similar effects, with a leaning to leadership, flashes of inventive thought and even genius. There is a greater emotional and nervous energy, which can sometimes be seen in a somewhat erratic enthusiasm.

Negative aspects are manifested as awkwardness and stubbornness, and the subject can be difficult, although this may be lessened by other factors.

Sun/Neptune aspects

In conjunction this aspect shows sensitivity and an intuitive nature. If there are no negative aspects influencing the chart, there may well be a creative flair. There can, however, often be a tendency towards the impractical, and the individual may be thought of as having his or her head in the clouds. Positive aspects create a vivid imagination that can be used to good effect, but it may also verge into daydreaming and thus become less productive than it might be.

Negative aspects may produce vagueness and muddled thinking and quite often there is a deceitful aspect to the nature, whether it applies to the self or others. The daydreaming feature of such individuals may become a definite drawback in that issues and reality are avoided.

Sun/Pluto aspects

A conjunction between the Sun and Pluto can tend to produce obsessive behaviour and considerable self-analysis. Depending on where the conjunction falls, however, it can enhance an intuitive individual. Positive aspects reinforce the theme of self-analysis, and this may be extended into an ability to undertake research.

Negative aspects, on the other hand, may prove very frustrating, with a likelihood of the individual being very reticent to talk through problems and situations, even with family members and close friends. Obsession is never far away but can be countered by other influences, particularly involving Venus and the Moon.

The Moon

Planets aspecting the Moon are subtly altered, and any matters ruled by that planet will probably undergo changes and modest alterations, heightening or lessening a particular characteristic.

Moon/Sun aspects—*see* section on The Sun.

Moon/Mercury aspects

A conjunction between the Moon and Mercury has a marked, positive mental effect, resulting in good instinctive behaviour that can extend into an active mind producing a facility for writing or something similar. Positive aspects produce common sense and the ability to work out a problem or situation and choose a logical solution.

Negative aspects can lead to a restless mind and an acrimonious nature, and although intellectual powers are heightened they may be used negatively, for example, in more gossip and criticism.

Moon/Venus aspects

The Moon in conjunction with Venus is a particularly good aspect, resulting in a balanced person who is calm, friendly and popular. It also has a positive effect on partnerships, making the individual very aware of his or her partner's needs. Positive aspects will show the same characteristics exhibited by a conjunction, with the additional benefits of intuition and charm.

Negative aspects may cause some difficulty in the outward expression of affections, and this can result in troubled relationships.

Moon/Mars aspects

The conjunction with Mars produces a strong influence and results in a tendency to be direct and energetic. However, it can also render someone too quick, and liable to jump first and check the ground afterwards. Positive aspects result in good physical and emotional strength, which means that the individual can make progress, whether in work or life generally.

Negative aspects lead to moodiness and a tendency to quarrel and also an impulsive nature that may lead to the necessary rescue of hastily made decisions.

Moon/Jupiter aspects

In conjunction these planets confer a helpful, kind nature to the individual, who is generally optimistic about events and often has a relatively trouble-free journey through life. Positive aspects have the same effect, particularly the trine, and the mental faculties are enhanced.

Negative aspects create a slightly destructive slant to these qualities so that the nature may be essentially the same, but judgement is affected and gains may be squandered.

Moon/Saturn aspects

A rather serious, cautious and even pessimistic outlook can be engendered by a conjunction between these planets. There is a desire for order and for things to be correct, so much so that the individual may be tagged a perfectionist. There may also be a timidness to the character and an underlying feeling of inadequacy, but loyalty can be relied upon.

Positive aspects include a commitment to duty willingly given and an ability to work reliably, thereby gaining a good reputation that is usually rewarded with progress. A lack of self-confidence, shyness and difficult relationships with the opposite sex all reflect negative aspects. If the individual is not careful it is quite easy for depression to take over, and other aspects of the chart should be studied to find more positive, constructive influences.

Moon/Uranus aspects

If the Moon and Uranus are in conjunction, there will be tension and emotions may be strained. Alongside the quite scintillating effects that may occur, there is a perversity and desire for the unusual, and often an independence in behaviour. Positive aspects result in a strong intuition and a need to achieve, which can be channelled constructively in almost any direction. Mood changes are common but are usually for the better.

Tension, an overpowering will, frequent (if only temporary) disagreements with friends all reflect the negative aspects. Flair and creativity may be present, but they need to be handled in the correct way.

Moon/Neptune aspects

Idealism, sensitivity and kindness all reflect a conjunction between the Moon and Neptune. These can be so dominant in the make-up that it can work to the subject's detriment should others take advantage of him or her. It is important to avoid deceptions that may be perpetrated in order that others are not hurt.

Positive aspects frequently add imagination to the character, but this must be controlled to avoid a muddled approach. A seriously muddled mind is typical of a negative aspect, as is the non-fulfilment of positive traits.

Moon/Pluto aspects

A conjunction between the Moon and Pluto commonly produces someone who is changeable and prone to highly emotional outbursts. Even so, this may act to his or her benefit in that a fresh start can be made uncluttered by bubbling discontent. It may, however, prove no easy task for the individual to express his or her true feelings if other planets restrict the conjunction.

Positive aspects create a similar tendency; outbursts may occur but can ultimately prove beneficial while the need to 'clear the decks' every so often will enable something or someone to be exorcised from the person. Negative aspects result in an inability to express oneself and open up emotionally, which can be frustrating and ultimately destructive unless countered elsewhere in the chart.

Mercury

Since Mercury is the planet of the mind, communication and general mental capacity, it is often feasible to find a positive outlet in this area.

Mercury/Sun aspects—*see* section on The Sun.

Mercury/Moon aspects—*see* section on The Moon.

Mercury/Venus aspects

In conjunction there will be an ease of mind rather than worry and a harmony and understanding of other people. A pleasant manner and charming speech result in good abilities to communicate. These planets are never separated by more than 76 degrees so the positive aspect that may be found is the sextile. This results in a friendly and affectionate nature and often an appreciation of, and ability in, craft pursuits.

The negative aspects may be the semi-sextile, which is very weak (and thus of little consequence), or the semi-square. The latter similarly has little adverse effect, save perhaps a critical manner, but depending on the configuration it may actually produce a greater balance of emotions in the character.

Mercury/Mars aspect

In conjunction with Mars, Mercury takes on the forceful, energetic nature of this planet. This produces someone who is mentally sharp, decisive and agile and able to take decisions quickly. Such individuals will probably prove effective in discussion or debate, which may serve them well in business. Aggressiveness may appear but will usually be manifested in strong opinions that the individual is quite happy to voice. Positive aspects produce much the same results with a lively mind but in addition an ability to handle stressful situations.

Negative aspects may result in moving too quickly, resulting in premature action, and incisiveness can become a more destructive carping. The mental faculties can be overloaded, resulting in tension and even a breakdown.

Mercury/Jupiter aspects

This conjunction confers very good mental creativity and potential, which may reflect a writer or any sort of literary occupation. There tends to be an appreciation of broader concepts rather than fine detail, although this will depend to a certain extent upon the remainder of the chart. A cheerful optimistic individual with a sense of humour reflects positive aspects, and in such cases challenges are necessary to stimulate the mind and obtain the best. Otherwise there may be a tendency to laziness.

In general, the negative aspects are not particularly problematical, but there can be carelessness if the mind is overloaded, or a tendency towards absent-mindedness.

Mercury/Saturn aspects

The conjunction of these two planets has a contradictory effect in that there is a mix of communication and limitation. It creates someone with a serious and thoughtful perspective on life, but he or she can become pessimistic. If combined with a good chart, there will be common sense and an attention to detail; conversely, a bad combination can result in mental slowness. Saturn will also inhibit and limit positive aspects, but there is often an enthusiastic nature combined with a useful reliability.

Negative aspects may force these characteristics to excess, causing obsessive behaviour in many ways, such as orderliness, self-discipline and depression.

Mercury/Uranus aspects

This conjunction is a particularly dynamic one and leads to a very quick mind, rich in inventive and innovative thought. It may also impart independence and a little stubbornness, and can produce an unconventional character who prefers the unusual and unorthodox. This is also seen with positive aspects, leading to originality and inventiveness, especially in a scientific context. Such individuals are self-assured and may be good with their hands.

The ability to communicate may become too sharp and almost isolated under the influence of negative aspects, and reaction to delays or difficult situations may be quite out of proportion to the problem faced. The preponderance of following the unusual can seem to others to be eccentric, which in itself becomes counterproductive.

Mercury/Neptune aspects

Mercury and Neptune in conjunction produce a fascinating result. The sensitivity and inspiration of Neptune confer on the individual a highly flexible mental attitude, resulting in creativity, intuition and a fertile imagination. There will not, however, necessarily be the rationalizing effect of common sense, and this may result in daydreaming. Positive aspects have a similar effect—sensitivity, kindness and an intuitive feel for people's aspirations and even thoughts.

Negative aspects lead to gullibility and unwillingness to face reality, and the thinking may operate in a scheming, deceptive way.

Mercury/Pluto aspects

The conjunction of Mercury with Pluto produces an individual capable of dispensing with worries easily and someone who enjoys the mental challenge of solving a mystery. A similar vein is seen with positive aspects, and there is a fascination and thoroughness when dealing with a topic that has once caught the individual's interest.

Negative aspects tend to be manifested as a secretive nature, perhaps with obsessive or stubborn sides to the character.

Venus

In general any planet aspected by Venus will be softened,

resulting in an enhancement of certain characteristics, such as the expression of love and dealing with possessions.

Venus/Sun aspects—*see* section on The Sun.

Venus/Moon aspects—*see* section on The Moon.

Venus/Mercury aspects—*see* section on Mercury.

Venus/Mars aspects

These two planets have a limiting effect on each other when in conjunction so that Mars limits the delicate beauty of Venus, and Venus limits the robust, coarse nature of Mars. As a result, the individual is enthusiastic, while sensitive to a partner's needs and also able to enjoy sexual relationships and all things of beauty. Positive aspects work in much the same way, with the further introduction of warmth into relationships.

Negative aspects may increase tension in relationships, often resulting in hurt and quarrels. If Venus is the stronger planet then the subject may be oversensitive to the comments of others.

Venus/Jupiter aspects

A conjunction between Venus and Jupiter is a very beneficial aspect and confers popularity, an artistic inclination and an affectionate nature. Such individuals work better in partnerships rather than alone and may lead a busy love life. Positive aspects produce similar results, and the individual will be popular, charming and happy.

Negative aspects tend not to be too detrimental because of the beneficial nature of both Venus and Jupiter. In most cases it will be an excess of a particular characteristic, thus the charm will be overplayed or an excessive number of love affairs will cause problems or there may be a discontent with being alone.

Venus/Saturn aspects

When Venus is in conjunction to Saturn there is often some

factor that inhibits the complete and open expression of affection or love, and this may produce disappointment in such affairs. There may also be a strong sense of duty, which, although it may bring its own rewards, can be traced back to strong inhibitions. Positive aspects tend to be less restrictive than the conjunction, and while there is a serious side to relationships, a particular partnership can benefit from faithfulness.

Negative aspects are also restrictive, to the point where it is difficult to express affection, although more positive characteristics elsewhere in the chart may help overcome this barrier.

Venus/Uranus aspects
In conjunction, these planets confer an element of inconsistency and an inability to focus the attention. In addition, emotions and tension may run high, and this really needs to be channelled and controlled. Although considerable personal appeal is possible, commitment may be lacking. Positive aspects lead to a less compulsive and magnetic personality and a tendency towards creativity and often considerable achievements.

The personality may retain its magnetism and dynamism, but under the influence of negative aspects there may also be a dramatic temper and impatience, which can cause nervous tension and strain.

Venus/Neptune aspects
There is a sensitivity and idealism when Venus is in conjunction with Neptune and an inclination towards pleasant or amiable behaviour. If the subject lives too much in the clouds, however, there will be self-delusion and a likelihood that partnerships and associations are not as solid and secure as perceived. When positive aspects are found, these will increase the chance of success, particularly in artistic pursuits such as music. Ideas and hunches may occur dur-

ing periods of apparent daydreaming, but in many cases these can prove more realistic than at first believed.

Negative aspects can produce problems, in that restlessness can turn to discontent if other areas of the chart reinforce this trait. There is a possibility of self-delusion unless common sense appears elsewhere, and confusion can occur in personal relationships.

Venus/Pluto aspects

The conjunction of Venus with Pluto is often a powerful one when it comes to emotions. It is quite likely that love will be felt deeply and passionately, but unless it is reciprocated there may be upheavals. Both planets influence money affairs, so this area may form a theme for a career. Positive aspects produce a very similar effect on personal relationships, especially those of the heart, while negative aspects tend to block these factors. The emotions may well be present, but there is an inability to talk above them and this can lead to frustration.

Mars

Mars will strongly affect any planet it contacts and will tend to create extremes in its positive and negative aspects.

Mars/Sun aspects—*see* section on The Sun.

Mars/Moon aspects—*see* section on The Moon.

Mars/Mercury aspects—*see* section on Mercury.

Mars/Venus aspects—*see* section on Venus.

Mars/Jupiter aspects

A conjunction between these two planets has very strong effects, resulting in energetic, decisive, enterprising individuals who tend not to miss opportunities. In addition, they will probably be willing to take on challenges that others would not even consider. There is a tendency for individuals to be almost daring, although they may be more argumentative. The influence of positive aspects is very good, leading to good humour, enthusiasm and the constructive taking of opportunities, whether physical, material or intellectual. Unless it is countered by controls shown elsewhere in the chart, the negative aspects can be quite destructive, with excesses in action and thought.

Mars/Saturn aspects

There tends to be something of a conflict when these planets are in conjunction, with Saturn limiting and Mars enlivening. As a result there may be mood swings from determination to frustration, from gloom to optimism. There may also be obstinacy. Positive aspects create a slightly more harmonious character such that the individual will be very determined. If put to good use this can lead to achievement in certain fields.

Negative aspects tend to result in a stern attitude, but this also means that hardships are endured. Selfishness is another trait that may be seen.

Mars/Uranus aspects

The combination of Mars and Uranus in conjunction produces very strong attributes, with determination, often obstinacy and frankness. Although this may not make the most pleasant of individuals, there will be a desire and ability to reach goals, but there may also be undue haste, which can result in accidents. Positive aspects confer independence and a magnetic character, but this may be a disadvantage unless used well. Flair and creativity can be manifested in engineering or science.

Tension and nervous strain result from negative aspects, and an argumentative nature is very likely. Personal relationships may be strained because of tactlessness, and an awareness of other people's feelings has to be engendered.

Mars/Neptune aspects

The conjunction of Mars with Neptune stimulates the imagination and strengthens the emotions. It can also make the individual somewhat lazy. In general there tends to be an interest in the arts, dancing and similar pursuits. Positive aspects lead to a creativity and original thinking that would be well employed in design. The emotional side of the individual is also enhanced.

Negative aspects can all too often result in escapist ways that can lead to problems. There may also be moodiness, and hard work undertaken possibly for perfectly altruistic motives may come to nought, perhaps because the idea had little substance at the outset.

Mars/Pluto aspects

An almost explosive nature can result when Mars is in conjunction to Pluto. Certainly there will be a determined, stubborn outlook, and it may be necessary to find a controlled outlet for the excessive energy. The temper is likely to be fierce, and obsessions are always possible. The character may even be flawed by a cruel streak. Hard work and ambition characterize the positive aspects, even to the point of the subject becoming a 'workaholic'.

Because both energy and emotions are increased by negative aspects, the subject may become someone who works almost obsessively to achieve a goal.

Jupiter

Jupiter's influence tends to be one of expansion and the provision of greater scope, and is often associated with understanding and knowledge.

Jupiter/Sun aspects—*see* section on The Sun.

Jupiter/Moon aspects—*see* section on The Moon.

Jupiter/Mercury aspects—*see* section on Mercury.

Jupiter/Venus aspects—*see* section on Venus.

Jupiter/Mars aspects—*see* section on Mars.

Jupiter/Saturn aspects

The conjunction of Jupiter with Saturn brings together seemingly opposing principles of limitation and expansion. If the influence of each is balanced, then common sense, a balanced approach to life and positive thinking will result. If the influences are not balanced there can be swings between optimism and pessimism, but in any event there is usually application to the task in hand and the ability to stay to the end. Positive aspects emphasize the constructive combination of common sense with optimism, producing a rounded character for whom little cannot be achieved. The intuition is good, as is their ability to plan and bring ideas to fruition.

Negative aspects introduce dissatisfaction and restlessness allied with a lack of self-confidence. There is also a tendency to press on regardless, even when caution is called for.

Jupiter/Uranus aspects

This conjunction produces an individual who is positive in his or her thinking, independent, and with a considerate approach to others. There may also be a good sense of humour, and such people are unlikely to be lost in the crowd. Many of these features are also produced by positive aspects, but in addition there is determination, self-belief and possibly an eccentricity bordering on genius.

Eccentricity can work to the individual's detriment under negative aspects, with an associated streak of pomposity. Such an individual may consider that everyone is wrong except he or she.

Jupiter/Neptune aspect

In conjunction these planets convey a kindness and desire to help others combined with idealism, although the effect of the latter trait will be shaped by the rest of the chart. In general there is optimism, and while there is a tendency to dream, a practical side should be sought. The positive aspects tend to be quite similar in effect, with an added altruism in their efforts.

The negative aspects often result in the beneficial qualities of kindness and sensitivity being overridden by lack of attention. In the extreme there may be escapism, foolishness or deception.

Jupiter/Pluto aspects

Jupiter in conjunction with Pluto produces a desire for power, material gain and an obsession in attaining goals. If it goes too far, it may verge on the fanatic, but if controlled these traits can prove very beneficial. The individual may well show leadership potential, and there may well be prominence in life at some time. Positive aspects provide similarly useful features, such as determination, the ability to lead and organize, and great strength of character.

The fanatical side of a character can develop under negative aspects, and if this is combined with an ability to lead and draw people, problems may arise. There may be a compulsion to gain what is wanted by violent means and to break away from existing constraints. Such tendencies must be tempered.

Saturn

A key feature of Saturn is its limiting effect, and this possibly relates to its being at the edge of the universe until late into the eighteenth century when the 'modern' planets were discovered.

Saturn/Sun aspects—*see* section on The Sun.

Saturn/Moon aspects—*see* section on The Moon.

Saturn/Mercury aspects—*see* section on Mercury.

Saturn/Venus aspects—*see* section on Venus.

Saturn/Mars aspects—*see* section on Mars.

Saturn/Jupiter aspects—*see* section on Jupiter.

Saturn/Uranus aspects

This conjunction has very great potential and, depending on the position of the conjunction, can result in great achievers. A practical outlook combined with persistence and other beneficial aspects can create brilliance. In certain circumstances the aspects can combine to produce someone with true leadership qualities, possibly a leader of their generation. There could always be nervous tension because of the conflict between limitation and freedom, which has to be countered. A balanced, perhaps more integrated, whole is generated by positive aspects, with persistence, patience and yet originality.

With negative aspects there may be a conflict, producing a stubborn nature and someone who is awkward and has a tendency to suffer from nervous tension.

Saturn/Neptune aspects

The conjunction of these two planets is interesting in that Uranus lies between the two for this period of the last generation, and this has a considerable effect. The overall result is an individual with a strong character who has ideas and imagination but controls them to the greatest benefit for all. There is a similar result with positive aspects, and in addition there is a kind and caring nature. An aptitude for science is not uncommon.

Negative aspects render these traits weaker, leading to confusion and a lack of application. There may be self-deprecation accompanied by shyness.

Saturn/Pluto aspects

Aspects involving these two planets occur rarely and last a long time when they do happen. The conjunction occurred last early in the 1980s when both planets were in Libra. This results in a determination allied with a pushing drive. Positive aspects confer a more determined outlook and also stubbornness.

Obsessional behaviour is typical of any negative aspects, and there is a tendency to avoid facing problems through misplaced fear, which makes the individual appear to waste time.

Uranus

Aspects between Uranus and the remaining planets Neptune and Pluto stay within orb for a long time (for example, from 1989 to 1998) because of the immense distances and separations involved and also the slow movement of Uranus. This means that such aspects will apply to the charts of people born within a long period.

Uranus/Sun aspects—*see* **section on The Sun.**

Uranus/Moon aspects—*see* **section on The Moon.**

Uranus/Mercury aspects—*see* **section on Mercury.**

Uranus/Venus aspects—*see* **section on Venus.**

Uranus/Mars aspects—*see* **section on Mars.**

Uranus/Jupiter aspects—*see* **section on Jupiter.**

Uranus/Saturn aspects—*see* **section on Saturn.**

Uranus/Neptune aspects

In conjunction there is the combination of independence, imagination and intuition with sensitivity, which produces an individual with inspirational qualities. Positive aspects often result in creatively or scientifically gifted people because logic, flair and similar attributes are strengthened.

Negative aspects may result in nervous tension, and the individual may be rather absent-minded. In such cases it is good practice to seek compensatory traits and activities elsewhere in the chart.

Uranus/Pluto aspects

This conjunction occurs very infrequently, roughly once

every 115 years, and because of the slow relative movement of the planets the effects are relevant for a generation. In many charts it will therefore not be a particularly strong feature. However, it may result in general frustration within the house in which the conjunction falls. Positive aspects may result in a likelihood to seek change while negative aspects can result in this trait being overdone and leading to disruptive behaviour.

Neptune

The majority of cases in which Neptune aspects with other planets have been covered in the preceding pages under the other planets. Just one planetary aspect remains.

Neptune/Pluto aspects

Because of the relationship between these two planets, conjunctions were formed many years ago but now Neptune is ahead of Pluto in their respective orbits around the Sun. As such a conjunction will not occur for some considerable time.

The only aspect that Neptune makes with Pluto is the sextile, and this occurs quite a lot in charts. Depending on the general construction of the chart, this may have little effect or it may strengthen intuition. However, the sextile is a weak aspect as other factors will tend to override it.

Aspects to the Ascendant and Midheaven

Other aspects that are important in interpreting charts are those between the planets and the ascendant and midheaven. In general, those to the ascendant have a personal implication while to the midheaven the implication applies to self-expression. It is essential that an accurate time of birth is known to allow a full interpretation. If this is not known, aspect to the ascendant and midheaven are better not included. The primary features and possibilities of these aspects are summarized below.

Sun / Ascendant aspects

Conjunction   rounded character, amiable; could be domineering, reticent.

Positive   depends on house position, but usually a strengthening effect.

Negative   depends on house but can be ambitious. Love of home but can be problematic.

Moon / Ascendant aspects

Conjunction   moody and often easily influenced. Secretive but intuitive.

Positive   good intuition, common sense with an adaptable character.

Negative   impatient and often discontented.

Mercury / Ascendant aspects

Conjunction   mentally sharp, versatile, communicative and imaginative.

Positive   similar to the conjunction.

Negative   tense and prone to worry and be over-talkative.

Venus / Ascendant aspects

Conjunction   affectionate and loving with an appreciation of things artistic. Care necessary not to overdo food or drink.

Positive   similar to the conjunction, with an understanding nature.

Negative   this may cause excesses in behaviour and personal relationships.

Mars / Ascendant aspects

Conjunction   a strengthening of physical or emotional energy. May be selfish but can be altruistic.

Positive   physically active, independent.

Negative   prone to quarrelling. May overdo things, for example, in work.

Jupiter / Ascendant aspects

Conjunction   depending upon the house, can be optimistic and lively but also fair-minded. May be a risk-taker.

Positive   effects similar to the conjunction.

Negative   may be prone to showing off to the detriment of relationships.

Saturn / Ascendant aspects

Conjunction   self-consciousness; practical with common sense nevertheless. Can be moody but also content, particularly in the home surroundings.

Positive   common sense and practical nature; also cautious.

Negative   may be pessimistic with a tendency to complain.

Uranus / Ascendant aspects

Conjunction   original and independent but can be irrational and nervous.

Positive   lively and creative usually with a need for independence.

Negative   unpredictable and possibly melodramatic.

Neptune / Ascendant aspects

Conjunction   variable effects but may include creativity, ill-discipline, or irrational behaviour.

Positive   quite inspired but may be tempered by forgetfulness.

Negative   possibly self-deceptive, and blinkered in situations where logic and analysis might be more appropriate.

Pluto / Ascendant aspects

Conjunction   strong emotions. May be secretive and prefer being' alone.

Positive   can be precipitate in actions; caution is required.

Negative   desire for change may become strong.

Sun / Midheaven aspects

Conjunction   ambitious and hopeful and usually self-confident. Can also be 'too big for their boots'.

Positive   ambitious but in a constructive way.

Negative   difficulty in achieving, great effort required.

Moon / Midheaven aspects

Conjunction   a strong character with possibility of leadership qualities.

Positive   a strengthening of traits associated with the sign containing the midheaven.

Negative   a dissatisfaction with life; dashed hopes or un-fulfilled dreams should be overcome with en-couragement.

Mercury / Midheaven aspects

Conjunction   highly communicative, can be applied to a career.
Positive   similar to the conjunction, also a balanced view of objectives.
Negative   may be prone to tension and worry.

Venus / Midheaven aspects

Conjunction   works well with people; considerate; may not have full powers of concentration and organization.
Positive   similar to the conjunction; more constructive effect than the conjunction for self-employed.
Negative   can be arrogant; prone to overreacting.

Mars / Midheaven aspects

Conjunction   thirst for success; energetically pursues the career.
Positive   enthusiastic, particularly in work.
Negative   hard-working but may be argumentative.

Jupiter / Midheaven aspects

Conjunction   content and optimistic; usually popular and fair. Can be successful, usually enthusiastic in what-ever venture is in hand.
Positive   good at meeting challenges, which enhances self-esteem. Optimistic and enthusiastic.
Negative   usually successful in a career but may exagger-ate, thereby losing standing with people around.

Saturn / Midheaven aspects

Conjunction   ambitious and can be high achievers; can han-dle responsibility but may let other aspects of life pass them by.

Positive	common sense and practicality; a good worker, who looks for promotion but reckless.
Negative	may experience frustration in reaching for goals; can be self-conscious and too cautious.

Uranus / Midheaven aspects

Conjunction	independent, perhaps with an inclination to rebellion, but may be creative and clever. Changes of direction possible, as is a liking for control.
Positive	similar to the conjunction, but with an innovative quality. The urge to change should be tempered, as it may become detrimental.
Negative	tension and a resultant over-caution may impede progress.

Neptune / Midheaven aspects

Conjunction	changes in direction may become frequent although this will not necessarily restrict progress.
Positive	imagination and flair will help appropriate careers.
Negative	liable to deceive, the subject may use dubious methods to achieve his or her aims.

Pluto / Midheaven aspects

Conjunction	a desire for influence may predominate. Careers may be marked by sudden, quite remarkable, changes of direction.
Positive	an ability to handle unexpected change.
Negative	life may throw up challenging situations with which some will cope and others not. It will all depend upon the remainder of the chart.

Constructing the Birth Chart

The construction of a birth chart is essentially a fairly elementary mathematical exercise. There are computer programs that enable it to be done simply, but in undertaking the task manually there is greater understanding and achievement.

Before beginning, a number of items are required:

- a blank chart; the one shown (*see* page 189) is of the equal house system. It can be drawn up quite easily using a pair of compasses.
- pen, pencil and ruler (and to begin with, probably an eraser).
- an atlas for determination of longitude and latitude.
- access to Raphael's ephemeris, which provides data on the position of the planet by month and year. Also known as the ephemerides, they are contained in some astrological books or you may have to consult a library. They are also available on computer.
- detailed instructions to follow or a computer program to use.

The following stages provide an overview of the process involved without complicated guidelines. It shows essentially how the data is derived but allows us to concentrate on the interpretive aspects of the subject.

Stage 1
The central horizontal line marks the horizon, and starting in the house below this line, the houses can be numbered 1 to 12, moving in an anticlockwise direction.

Stage 2

The position of the ascendant is now calculated. There are a number of calculations to be made, but the first task is to determine the longitude and latitude of the place of birth. The time of birth is also vital and should initially be stated as the birth time in Greenwich Mean Time. To find the ascendant and mid-heaven, the birth time is converted to sidereal time (that is, in relation to the stars) with minor adjustments for the year. Because the sidereal time from the tables relates to midnight it must be changed to the sidereal time at the time of birth by adding the sidereal time to the time of birth. Again, minor amendments have to be made at this point, both for minor changes in sidereal time and the precise geographical location of the place of birth. Again, tables are used for this latter correction. This calculation produces a true sidereal time of birth, and by referring to a *table of houses*, degree values can be found for the ascendant and midheaven.

In this example the ascendant is 22 degrees Cancer and the midheaven is 20 degrees Pisces. Referring back to the chart, the 22 degrees are counted clockwise around the chart from the horizon line and the ascendant is marked. This is the cusp (that is, junction) of the first sign, and the remaining sign divisions can be drawn in from here, every 30 degrees around the chart. The glyphs of the sign are then added and the midheaven is also positioned.

Stage 3

The next stage is to determine the positions of the Sun, Moon and other planets. By reference to the ephemerides, the positions can be found, and these are given as a number of degrees in a particular sign. The example here results in the following, rounded to the nearest degree for simplicity:

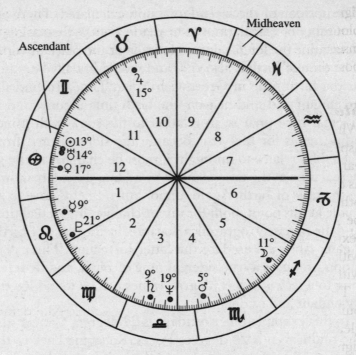

The birth chart with initial placings of the ascendant,
midheaven and planets

Sun	13 degrees	Cancer
Moon	11 degrees	Sagittarius
Mercury	9 degrees	Leo
Venus	17 degrees	Cancer
Mars	5 degrees	Scorpio
Jupiter	15 degrees	Taurus
Saturn	9 degrees	Libra
Uranus	14 degrees	Cancer
Neptune	19 degrees	Libra
Pluto	21 degrees	Leo

Each planet is now marked on the chart in the relevant sign, counting anticlockwise from the sign division. Each plot should be marked and the appropriate planetary glyph inserted. The chart, completed to this point, is shown opposite with all information calculated to date.

Stage 4

When the planetary positions have been established, the aspects can be determined. As described earlier, there are various aspects that may be apparent, and when constructed as described their significance can be determined from the other sections of the book. On the sample chart there can be seen conjunctions (the Sun with Venus and Uranus), sextiles (the Sun, Uranus and Venus, all with Jupiter; Pluto with Neptune), squares (Neptune with Venus and the Moon with Saturn), and so on.

The complete picture of a chart, and the personality, is built up from information such as this but also the details gleaned from the position of the planets with respect to the signs and houses. The Sun's sign influence has already been covered in reasonable detail, and below the remaining planets are dealt with. It is possible to give only the briefest indication of influences here, but more comprehensive details will be found in other publications. The next section therefore deals with the planets through the signs and houses, beginning with the Sun through the houses.

The Planets through the Houses

The Sun

The energy of the Sun is very important, and it shows by its house position in which facet of life the energy will be focused.

The Sun in the . . .

. . . First house

Indicates the strong, self-centred type who is good at giving orders—and may therefore be successful in business—but not so good at taking them.

. . . Second house

Very acquisitive, both in terms of money and other possessions and with a desire to flaunt it a little. This may also apply to a partner, that is, the partner is also regarded as a possession. The motivation may be a wish to be wealthy or a fear of being poor.

. . . Third house

At whatever level, the mind will be active and the person will be a communicator.

. . . Fourth house

Seeks the security of a good home and happy family life, and may also work from home.

. . . Fifth house

Creativity needs to be expressed and enjoyment will be

gained from that. Spontaneous and proud but generous and may be upset easily. There is a desire to feel important and wanted.

. . . Sixth house

Such people are hard workers and often commit themselves to the local community, or their employer and, of course, their family. Personal health is a feature of this house, whether for good or bad, but it may also show as employment or voluntary work in the health sector.

. . . Seventh house

Relationships with others become very important whether it is on a personal level or concerned with work. Emotional dependence may actually become a problem.

. . . Eighth house

An interest in self-development, which may relate to money or the personality. Strong emotional tendencies with a perceptive mind.

. . . Ninth house

Education and travel are both associated with this house and both help to broaden the mind. There is a strong desire to learn and possibly to teach.

. . . Tenth house

A strong commitment to ambition, work (may actually overdo work) and possessions, with a desire for progress in a career. Secure family life is also important.

. . . Eleventh house

Is drawn to cooperative ventures, working with other people and is often a good communicator. Very close relationships are however often avoided.

. . . Twelfth house

Tends to like quiet and seclusion but can be creative. The

most withdrawn of all the houses. Usually wants to improve life for others even though the subject may have no great ambition for himself or herself.

The Moon in the . . .

. . . First house

A natural instinct to care for others but not to the detriment of self-interest. Likes travelling. Is susceptible to mood changes.

. . . Second house

There is a need for security through money and possessions and often a desire to collect the latter. Emotions will affect judgement on money.

. . . Third house

Usually a good communicator and often turns to teaching. Shrewd but could be a deceiver. Intelligent and humorous but commonly restless and always on the move.

. . . Fourth house

A strong feeling exists for the home and family and a safe, solid base is essential. Caring and protective in nature, but may become obsessive and retiring.

. . . Fifth house

An outlet for creativity is vital, which may manifest itself in parenthood. Socially active and may be something of an extrovert but with quick reversals of mood.

. . . Sixth house

Good workers who often opt for charity work or the health field. Emotions frequently affect health and work.

. . . Seventh house

Usually look for close emotional ties, although in so doing their individuality may be lost. Subject to mood swings. Job variety and interest is sought.

. . . Eighth house

Emotional and intuitive, often to the point where they have a 'sixth sense'. Usually a good business sense. Strong sexual needs.

. . . Ninth house

An interest in things foreign, be it travel, language or culture. Also a tendency for higher education and for religion.

. . . Tenth house

An ability to lead and a desire for status and power. An understanding of those being led, which can lead to being highly esteemed.

. . . Eleventh house

Tends to get involved in activities involving groups, which they themselves may lead. Politics commonly appeals.

. . . Twelfth house

Time alone is always valued. In working for others it is usually 'behind the scenes'.

Mercury in the . . .

. . . First house

Talkative and quick-witted with some nervousness. Versatile and keen to learn and to present own ideas. May be prone to excessive worry.

. . . Second house

Financially astute with an aptitude for financial dealings and the creation of wealth.

. . . Third house

Usually communicative and often employed in a profession where such skills can be used. Mentally agile with an interest in education.

. . . Fourth house

The home is particularly important and may base work

there. Interest in the family and its past and history generally. Can be restless.

. . . Fifth house

Highly creative in a literary or craft pursuit although may be lacking in attention to detail. Generally at ease with children, something that is usually reciprocated.

. . . Sixth house

Excellent at communication and in analysing situations and problems. Makes a good employee, working carefully, and also a good employer who maintains an interest in employees, their health, etc.

. . . Seventh house

Seeks a sharing, caring relationship whether in marriage or pastimes. Can be a good business person with an ability to act as intermediary. Often interested in other's problems but not necessarily out of totally altruistic motives.

. . . Eighth house

May have an interest in mysterious things, for example, psychic phenomena, but can also prove to have a good business sense. An enquiring mind with good powers of concentration.

. . . Ninth house

A thirst for knowledge and understanding is very strong and may lead to a career in research with considerable academic achievements. Also may have an aptitude for languages.

. . . Tenth house

Variety is necessary, particularly in the career, and there may be changes in career direction. Generally a good approach to business, although financial reward is not necessarily the primary motivation.

... Eleventh house

A very friendly type who enjoys social contact and the opportunity to discuss ideas. This may lead to involvement in local groups, organizations or politics.

... Twelfth house

Tends to be emotional and shy, almost secretive and lacking a little in self-confidence.

Venus in the ...

... First house

An attractive and charming character, which in part is a means to securing friendship. Kind and sympathetic, often interested in the outward appearance, that is, fashion and beauty.

... Second house

Likes to collect possessions, especially things of value and beauty. A competent approach to business in the main, but this is often used to impress.

... Third house

Very friendly and sociable with an ability to communicate effectively. Welcomes a mental challenge.

... Fourth house

The home is central and is a focus of pride. Every attempt is made to make it nice and secure and comfortable. Dislikes arguments and can be quite effective at defusing situations likely otherwise to end in quarrels.

... Fifth house

Likes luxury and glamour and participating in social events. Gets on well with children. Creative with an affinity for the arts.

. . . Sixth house

The working environment must be pleasing and conducive to work. A steady pace in all things is ideal. Socially correct and critical of those who are not.

. . . Seventh house

An interesting combination of shrewdness and affection. Often popular with their peers, they can sometimes rely too much on a partner and make unreasonable requests.

. . . Eighth house

An increase in emotions and sexual matters can be uplifting or totally problematic. Generally sympathetic but can become jealous and secretive.

. . . Ninth house

A strong interest in other cultures with a desire for foreign travel, which may lead to residence or even marriage abroad. Varied contacts in social circles with a relaxed attitude in general.

. . . Tenth house

Socially adept with positive spin-off in the career, forming good relationships with work colleagues.

. . . Eleventh house

Large number of social contacts and an enjoyment of communal ventures, fund-raising, etc. Good organizer of events.

. . . Twelfth house

Shy and incommunicative with secretive emotional feelings.

Mars in the . . .

. . . First house

Very energetic and positive although sometimes impulsive and even hot-headed. They usually put themselves first although can be very helpful to others.

... Second house

A desire to build up possessions and wealth but often an extravagant spender. Very competitive in business and may be likely to take risks.

... Third house

Competitive and often argumentative. Also inquisitive and may have a temper. In being argumentative, they may also lack tact.

... Fourth house

Much effort is spent on the home in decoration and improvements. On occasion restlessness may precipitate moving home.

... Fifth house

Energetic in all aspects of life whether social, creative or romantic. A keen sportsperson who enjoys leisure time. Tends to be good with children but often pressurizes his or her own children to succeed.

... Sixth house

A hard worker who gets on with the task in hand. Quite ambitious and competitive but can be rather impatient when faced with delays. They will also be difficult when disagreeing with colleagues.

... Seventh house

Forceful in partnerships and can prove argumentative. Can be popular through their energetic participation but they can offend or upset people through their outspoken nature.

... Eighth house

Interest in investigative work or financial occupations. Highly intuitive. Strong sex drive.

... Ninth house

Adventurous and interested in travel. Also intellectually very capable and may find education rewarding. Usually have strongly held views and beliefs.

. . . Tenth house

A very strong character and a hard worker, which in regard to the career means ambition, success and an achiever. Although they make good employers, they can on occasion be a little too ruthless.

. . . Eleventh house

Likely to get involved in various groups and organizations where they will probably become leaders. Friends are important but their basically argumentative nature may cause temporary rifts.

. . . Twelfth house

A desire to help others, perhaps in the caring professions but often working behind the scenes. Can become secretive, too much so, which leads to problems not being discussed and solved.

Jupiter in the . . .

. . . First house

Honest, optimistic and generally outgoing with a tendency to offer encouragement to others. A possible weakness may be overconfidence.

. . . Second house

Money is a central theme although the emphasis may vary. In some, money is made effortlessly while in others it is of secondary importance. Generous in partnerships and with a desire for comfort in the home.

. . . Third house

Welcomes mental challenges, shares ideas and opinions but may force them on others. Can be restless but there is often a desire to continue in education, possibly through self-teaching.

. . . Fourth house

Strong ties with the family and home life and may have ambition for a large house.

. . . Fifth house

Enthusiastic and optimistic, and may also be creative. Generally self-confident but in excess this can lead to risk-taking and someone who shows off.

. . . Sixth house

Helpful and generous and particularly so in work when a good rewarding job will take precedence over the financial return.

. . . Seventh house

Friendly and quick to form new contacts, although sometimes with an ulterior motive. Good in business and assertive, with plenty of ideas for development.

. . . Eighth house

Often a good business person who invests wisely. Can be over-demanding where a partner is concerned and may also like freedom to the detriment of a relationship.

. . . Ninth house

May have an interest in travel and foreign cultures. There is also a continuing desire to find out, acquire knowledge or study. Can become self-opinionated.

. . . Tenth house

An ability to grasp the significance of situations and take a long-term view. Tend to work towards their goals, becoming wiser en route. Can be rather melodramatic with a tendency to show off.

. . . Eleventh house

Very sociable with many superficial friends and acquaintances, and just a few real friends. Quick to offer encouragement and provide ideas.

. . . Twelfth house

Can be rather idealistic, finding the material world unsatisfactory. Prefer in many cases to work alone although they will have an excellent mind.

Saturn in the . . .

. . . First house

Shy and lacking self-confidence although with common sense and responsibility. Can often meet with repeated setbacks but through dogged perseverance can succeed.

. . . Second house

Works hard to make the money that is gained but little comes easily in this respect. There may be a tendency to possessiveness, and over-caution can lead to lost opportunities.

. . . Third house

Success usually comes later in life through sheer hard work as a lack of confidence is overcome. Usually practical-minded and sensible with a caring attitude to brothers and sisters.

. . . Fourth house

A potentially unhappy early life may link at a later stage with the need for domestic security. Intuitive, although the individual may have to learn to accept intuitive judgements.

. . . Fifth house

A latent creativity may need to be encouraged. May find dealing with children difficult, possibly because of their own childhoods.

. . . Sixth house

Usually committed to hard work, although possibly in a

complaining way, but goals are commonly met. Avoidance of change. May be excessively concerned about their health.

. . . Seventh house

Regards partnerships very seriously and may choose an older partner, but tends to be very faithful. Occasionally there will be problems in relationships.

. . . Eighth house

A generally serious perspective on life, with the potential for depression. Very good at financial pursuits, particularly in their responsible attitude to the money of other people, thus suited to banking or insurance.

. . . Ninth house

Thinks seriously and sensibly about important matters, but with a conventional, traditional approach to most matters. There is a tendency to travel, although in some this raises problems and even phobias.

. . . Tenth house

Ambitious, with high hopes and an ability to take responsibility. These people make good, dependable workers who can progress through hard work, overcoming difficulties on the way.

. . . Eleventh house

Hard-working and often a little shy. However, a definite effort may be made to be more sociable, which frequently results in membership of numerous committees. A concern for all good causes is evident.

. . . Twelfth house

Can withdraw into his or her own world but in any event will welcome the security of home. Good, supportive workers in whatever they do.

Uranus in the . . .

. . . First house
Intelligent, freedom-loving and individualistic, so much so that they may prefer competition to cooperation. Quite unpredictable, but original and often brilliant.

. . . Second house
This has financial implications and may result in the unexpected gain or loss of money. Can be emotionally cool with a possessive streak.

. . . Third house
Original and mentally alert and likely to respond negatively to the orthodox system of education. Seeks logical answers to problems, can be inventive. A stubborn, awkward streak may also be apparent.

. . . Fourth house
A rather perverse, mixed-up influence with the subject wanting a stable secure home life but also considerable freedom. They may be brilliant but moody. However, it is best to encourage and develop the intuitive ideas of such a person.

. . . Fifth house
A creative individual with flair and originality. Their children tend to be clever but may be demanding. Emotionally rather fearless, these people will often take risks.

. . . Sixth house
May experience health problems, perhaps associated with tension. There is an affinity for work that is slightly out of the ordinary and that requires invention, flair or idealism.

. . . Seventh house
Relationships are affected greatly. Often the individual will not want to be tied down and partners need to be very understanding. There may be mixed emotions about such ties that can lead to mistakes, although there can be a generally romantic outlook.

. . . Eighth house

Commonly a relaxed attitude to money, which may result in unpredictable actions that subsequently cause friction. Fickle sexually and possibly obsessive in analysing problems.

. . . Ninth house

Often clever with a flair for science or the arts and an appetite for challenges. Travel is sought with possible attraction for a foreign culture resulting.

. . . Tenth house

Career direction may change abruptly, particularly if there is not the scope for their talents. Not averse to holding positions of power, leadership is handled well.

. . . Eleventh house

Superficially friendly with a varied social life and often a hard-working commitment to a cause or organization. Dislikes inaction and lethargy in others.

. . . Twelfth house

Highly imaginative, often in a strange way with an interest in the unusual or mysterious. Often takes to a humanitarian cause to the detriment of a personal relationship.

Neptune in the . . .

. . . First house

Imaginative and sensitive with a tendency to daydream. In general such people are kind and unselfish, but may be rather gullible.

. . . Second house

A potentially varied and unpredictable attitude to money including a susceptibility to be misled. May be sentimental and loving.

. . . Third house

Imaginative and communicative, particularly with respect

to artistic careers or pastimes. May achieve later rather than sooner through lack of application in the early years of education.

. . . Fourth house

Chaos may reign at home in both organization and general provision of domestic routine but also in giving guidance to children. Usually imaginative and a lover of animals.

. . . Fifth house

Creative, with imagination. Romantic associations can be a little too consuming and would benefit from a wise head.

. . . Sixth house

Can be attracted to work in the caring professions but may not be very good at meeting deadlines. Tend to be self-sacrificing and often work hard for little recompense but can be impractical at times. Health may be a problem, particularly with allergies.

. . . Seventh house

Too much may be expected romantically, and disappointment may result, or there may be a tendency to rush in without considering the implications.

. . . Eighth house

Romantic/sexual activities can be quite dominant. In money matters there will be generosity, but the individual may prove easily led, perhaps by a business partner.

. . . Ninth house

Inspired and imaginative with a fascination for other cultures and mysticism. May find a career in religion. Travel often features strongly.

. . . Tenth house

An idealist and romantic, which in a career can lead to unrealistic hopes or success if the idealism can be used to good effect. There are likely to be many changes of emphasis and direction in life.

. . . Eleventh house
Sociable but not very perceptive in such circumstances. There may be some shyness and an aversion to taking on responsibility as this can result in stress.

. . . Twelfth house
Kind and caring, which may be reflected in the choice of career where they can readily understand the problems of other people. Often creative with an affinity for the arts.

Pluto in the . . .

. . . First house
Strong and dynamic with a determination to work hard and achieve targets. Can also be moody and obsessive with an emotional intensity. Strongly developed motivation with an excellent ability to bounce back after setbacks.

. . . Second house
There is usually a good aptitude for business and money matters, which when allied with a determination to succeed can lead the individual to considerable success. An intense emotional life, although may be manipulative.

. . . Third house
Can be very good at communicating although often the urge to be quiet and contemplative masks this. Perceptive and curious, which may lead to a career in research.

. . . Fourth house
Strong feelings about the home although there may be concealed frustration from his or her early life. Intuitive, and this will help deal with any emotional or family problems.

. . . Fifth house
Usually creative and with a determination to use their potential to the full. Too much may be expected of romantic/emotional associations.

. . . Sixth house

A disciplined individual who works hard and to a routine if applicable and may be rather hard on himself or herself. May experience health problems.

. . . Seventh house

An aptitude for the financial aspects of a business. Can appreciate others, with understanding and sympathy, but must be careful not to dominate a partner.

. . . Eighth house

A good business sense. Intuitive and logical but may experience sexual problems.

. . . Ninth house

Frequently shows connection with or interest in foreign countries and different faiths. Seeks mental challenge. Quite a strong personality.

. . . Tenth house

A strong desire to succeed, which may be shown in the career, where personal power will be sought. An interest also in money and politics. May be ruthless.

. . . Eleventh house

A tendency to become involved in groups or societies, and possibly in politics. There may, however, be a predominance of these interests over domestic concerns, to the detriment of the latter.

. . . Twelfth house

A likelihood that the individual will be secretive, whether in financial or romantic matters. Habitually searching and analysing, which may be directed on themselves.

The Planets through the Signs

The positions of the planets with respect to the Zodiac signs are unique for each chart. Each planet has twelve expressions through the signs, which follow a basic pattern, so in Aries, planets act assertively and powerfully.

The planets in Aries

Moon
Quick in reaction, thought and temper and rather impulsive. Can be good partners but may also be selfish.

Mercury
Quick-thinking and strong-willed with an enjoyment of debate. Decisive and to the point.

Venus
Affectionate, even passionate, with a generous nature. Lively socially and generally popular.

Mars
Energetic, even aggressive, and usually leading the way. They can be impulsive and obstinate although friendly, and they may create problems through carelessness.

Jupiter
Optimistic and enthusiastic with a love of freedom. Can be generous, but these traits to excess can lead to recklessness and extravagance.

Saturn
Assertive and strong, and very determined, thus more than able to cope when circumstances become difficult.

Uranus

Originality with self-confidence, although there may be impatience and a tendency to behave foolishly.

Neptune

This is an impossible placing because of the slow motion of Neptune.

Pluto

The same applies as for Neptune.

The planets in Taurus

Moon

A solid base is required to counter any emotional ups and downs, but otherwise very practical with lots of common sense.

Mercury

Stubborn but with an ability to consider problems of a practical nature and work steadily. Generally cheerful.

Uranus

Warm and affectionate and generally faithful. Likes craft and the arts, including music. Aims for financial security, through hard work if necessary.

Mars

Quick-tempered and passionate. Such individuals work very hard and can be very determined, almost stubborn. Works at making money.

Jupiter

Appreciates good living and usually has the flair and good judgement to use and invest money well. Generous but can be possessive.

Saturn

Very patient, with caution and discipline, but can become too stubborn. Ambitious and materialistic.

Uranus

Stubborn yet sound and with some flair. May be erratic with money, splashing out and then saving every penny.

Neptune

This placing cannot occur for living subjects because of the slow orbit of Neptune.

Pluto

The same applies as for Neptune.

The planets in Gemini

Moon

Quick to respond and versatile. There is a reluctance to get too involved emotionally. Can be impatient and restless.

Mercury

A desire to communicate and exchange ideas. A quick thinker, decision maker and quite inventive. Can be impatient with slower people but adaptable.

Venus

A good communicator and a lively personality. Can be flirtatious but often avoids emotional ties through constant analysis and thus does not face the real issues. May be restless.

Mars

A good mind but has a tendency to take on too much, thereby reducing effectiveness. Usually versatile and capable but can be nervous and impatient.

Jupiter

Inventive and clever but can skip from one area to another and grasp only superficial knowledge Often takes to teaching as communication is good.

Saturn

Good mind with a logical approach to problems. May be a

late developer and generally good at the physical sciences computing, mathematics, etc.

Uranus
A quick thinker who has original and often brilliant ideas. However, he or she may be nervous and tense.

Neptune
Very few people will have Neptune in Gemini, unless very old.

Pluto
Applies only to the elderly (born before 1912).

The planets in Cancer

Moon
Highly instinctive, emotional and affectionate. A secure, stable home life is very important, and these individuals are adept at homemaking. Can be moody and a little possessive.

Mercury
Kind and thoughtful with a good imagination. Intuition and opinions are strong, as is the dislike of change. A good memory is not unusual.

Venus
Sympathetic and affectionate, but if overdone can be possessive and clinging. They love the home and make it as comfortable as possible and are likely to make sensible investments.

Mars
Great commitment, physical and emotional, to see things through. Although they need security and a strong family life, they are ambitious. Occasionally very short-tempered.

Jupiter
Kind and sympathetic, and also dutiful. Quite good at busi-

ness and generally ambitious on behalf of and for the family.

Saturn

Can be self-pitying and suspicious, and there is a need for emotional stability. May be a worrier, but there is also a financial aptitude and general shrewdness. Hard-working and ambitious.

Uranus

Imaginative and original though logical. Can be moody and unpredictable and difficult to work with.

Neptune

This placing occurred in the early years of the twentieth century. It confers intuition and sensitivity although the individual may be too imaginative and prone to worry.

Pluto

Generally emotionally strong and intuitive. Can be a good business person with staying power, although some may fall prey to excessive worry.

The planets in Leo

Moon

Confident and with a desire to impress, but can be self-centred. Enthusiastic and lively but may, in their ambition, start taking over. Can be stubborn and difficult.

Mercury

Creative and well organized in a practical sense. A good communicator but can be arrogant and patronizing. Generally happy and with a positive outlook.

Venus

Lively, generous and faithful, this person will adore his or her partner and will love children and material things. May be a tendency to show off and be extravagant.

Mars

Looks for leadership because of organizational ability and enthusiasm. Socially active with a touch of drama that can be overdone. May be too pushy and overbearing.

Jupiter

Usually generous and enthusiastic with a positive outlook on life. Can also be ambitious but melodramatic and over-powering.

Saturn

Determined, well-organized and faithful apply here. Can often be bossy and arrogant, especially if they are pursuing a long-held goal.

Uranus

Quite dynamic, which can result in good leadership quali-ties. However, there will almost certainly be stubbornness. Often creative but with mixed personal outlook on rela-tionships.

Neptune

Enthusiastic and creative with a good imagination. Com-monly an interest in the visual arts, such as photography or film.

Pluto

May succeed in business through flair rather than calcula-tion. Interested in technology. Commonly shows leadership qualities although occasionally these may degenerate into empire-building tendencies.

The planets in Virgo

Moon

A strong tendency to be well-ordered, neat and with a dis-like of bad behaviour. Can be lacking in self-confidence and a worrier but with a practical streak.

Mercury

An analytical mind and practical, which makes these people good at solving problems. May become bogged down in detail when wanting to be precise but generally able to cope with demanding tasks.

Venus

Often shy and with few close friends, perhaps because they tend to be critical of other people, often due to their own lack of self-confidence. Good at business and communicating.

Mars

A hard worker who pays attention to detail but lacks imagination. The emotions and personal relationships may not run too smoothly.

Jupiter

Patient but can be overconcerned with detail, critical but kind. There may be worry and mental conflict when facing a problem because of lack of self-confidence. Tends to be kind and matter-of-fact.

Saturn

Patient, modest, with attention to detail and duty. Hard work is not avoided and personal standards are kept high. Can be too hard on others, for example, employees, and may be a little detached from others.

Uranus

Can lead to originality but the familiar is not rejected. Depending upon other placings, the individual can be dynamic and somewhat restless.

Neptune

Imaginative and expressive, but there may be a lack of self-confidence and an associated dissatisfaction.

Pluto

An ability to see, grasp and solve problems, although some

individuals may find difficulty in talking about their own worries. Can be very critical of others.

The planets in Libra

Moon
Sympathetic and understanding, to the point where they will help to sort out problems for other people. Clear thinkers, very charming but can be moody.

Mercury
Peace-loving, sympathetic, can see many possibilities, but this can leave them indecisive. Gentle and affectionate. Often good at business but will need application and discipline.

Venus
Kind and understanding, and tactful in helping others with a dislike of argument. Quite generous with money but fond of luxuries. May be lazy and indecisive.

Mars
Affectionate, keen to promote and maintain unity, but can themselves be argumentative. Perceptive and friendly.

Jupiter
Sympathetic, kind and generous; a naturally warm person. Has a relaxed attitude to life with a love of luxuries that can lead to self-indulgence.

Saturn
Understanding with a feeling for what is right and wrong, kind and fair. May be some intolerance and difficulty with relationships.

Uranus
Friendly and caring, and unselfish when someone is in need. May be independent and unsure of being committed to a partnership.

Neptune
Sympathetic, peace-loving and kind. May be lacking in self-confidence and self-deceiving.

Pluto
A tendency to start arguments, particularly with a partner to prove a point. Can be jealous.

The planets in Scorpio

Moon
Very emotional and may be jealous. Determined with a strong ambitious urge. Tend to be a little retiring socially but in personal relationships can be very committed.

Mercury
Intuitive with a logical mind although can be obsessional and possessive. Usually loyal in relationships.

Venus
Passionate, possessive with occasional jealousy. Often a flair for business, investment and money, but obstinacy could interfere.

Mars
Full of potential with a strong character. Hard-working with ambitions but self-discipline may be lacking. Perceptive with, occasionally, a critical nature. Can be secretive but with strong motivation and commitment.

Jupiter
Determined, with a will to succeed, especially in the career. Lives a full life but in many cases may need to ease off a little.

Saturn
Committed to goals, determined and with a very good ability in business. Can be ruthless, stubborn and obstinate, and consideration should be encouraged if they are to succeed.

Uranus

Emotional but afraid to show it, courageous and may take risks. May be a liking for power but potential must be developed in the correct direction.

Neptune

Emotional, but can be ambitious and even inspiring if this is also shown elsewhere in the chart. May be fortuitous with money.

Pluto

A desire to make money and achieve a powerful position in some way. Usually strong emotions and quite intuitive.

The planets in Sagittarius

Moon

A liking for freedom and also travel, which may result in living abroad. A challenge is always enjoyed, and the individual is enthusiastic and positive with a desire to maintain progress. May be restless and a little offhand.

Mercury

Can be unrealistic and superficial but, on the positive side, will always be learning, and is broad-minded. Grasps situations quickly, versatile.

Venus

Emotional freedom is required, and may not like to be tied. Idealistic and imaginative but may be thoughtless.

Mars

Very ambitious, often on a grand scale. Very energetic and independent but with a non-traditional approach. Can be argumentative and heavy-handed.

Jupiter

Enthusiastic and positive with a tendency to look for intellectual development. Often intuitive and with a good sense of judgement.

Saturn
Study is a primary aim, assisted by a capacity for concentration. Honest and forthright, these people will not be afraid to challenge the thinking of the majority.

Uranus
Original in thought and welcomes a challenge, caring in an altruistic sense and with this is a good sense of humour.

Neptune
Generally understanding and caring with an idealistic streak. Also enthusiastic and positive-thinking.

Pluto
This occurs only from 1995 until well beyond the millennium. Likely to be independent and generally sensible, possibly wise.

The planets in Capricorn

Moon
Unable to show feelings easily and may find partnerships difficult although good at homemaking. Ambitious to some extent but with a tendency towards arrogance, but with a good sense of humour.

Mercury
Down to earth, practical and to the point. Determined and careful, but can be restless. Often a tendency to scientific pursuits.

Venus
Tends to stick with tradition and conventional relationships. Good in business with a careful approach, although occasionally showing off.

Mars
Very ambitious, seeking targets, and with a liking for power. Generally practical-minded but can be stubborn and cold.

Jupiter
A good worker who sees the job through. Very sensible and responsible, with ambition and reliability. Can be stubborn.

Saturn
Ambitious, practical, hard-working and well-organized. May like power. Can be pessimistic and likely to complain, but has a good sense of humour.

Uranus
A careful thinker but with occasional lapses. There may be a hard side to the character, which could be tempered by a concern for good causes.

Neptune
Possibly creative. Determined and positive with a cautious streak but may be subject to self-deception.

Pluto
It is unlikely that this placing will be found.

The planets in Aquarius

Moon
Independent, dislike of being tied down emotionally and may reject the responsibilities of a home. There is a strength of character but also an awkwardness and unpredictability. Often original with a flash of brilliance.

Mercury
Like freedom, both physical and intellectual. Tend to be intuitive and inventive, often with radical views. May be stubborn and critical but very good with humanitarian causes.

Venus
Tends to value freedom, even in personal relationships, which can cause problems. Kind and caring and usually good with money.

Mars
Original thinker and intellectual but can be impulsive. Idealistic but more often than not impractical. Can be erratic and stubborn.

Jupiter
Imaginative, evenhanded, idealistic and fair. Such people have many good qualities, such as understanding, warmth, cheerfulness. There may occasionally be tactlessness and unpredictability.

Saturn
Independent and an original thinker with determination and ambition. There can be a tendency to change suddenly and an obstinate streak. Often good with scientific pursuits.

Uranus
Friendly and caring, supporting good causes. Quite innovative and independent. Likely to be unpredictable.

Neptune
This placing will be found only from the last year or two of this century.

Pluto
It is unlikely that this placing will be found.

The planets in Pisces

Moon
Caring, sympathetic, very helpful and hospitable but tend to be vulnerable. This means that although they have a great deal to offer, they may find the real world a little harsh.

Mercury
Intuitive, sympathetic, caring and with a desire to help others. However can be forgetful and lacking in confidence.

Venus
Very emotional and sentimental. May be gullible and eas-

ily deceived. Relationships may flounder between the realities and the hopes, or fantasies.

Mars
Imaginative and intuitive, but generally quite impractical even though creative. Gentle and artistic but lacks commitment.

Jupiter
Sympathetic and understanding and able to get on well with others. Imaginative and yet needs targets to aim for. Can be self-indulgent or subject to self-deception.

Saturn
Intuitive, idealistic and imaginative with a flair for creative outlets. However, such people tend to be shy and inhibited, and there is often a tendency to worry.

Uranus
Idealistic, caring but especially with an originality and inventiveness that may be truly inspired. May follow the crowd, even into trouble, but generally this can be overcome.

Neptune
This will not be found.

Pluto
This will not be found.

Birthday Calendar

The following birthday calendar gives guidance for the future tendencies of each birth date. Use it in conjunction with the given characteristics for each sign.

January

1 Seize any opportunities that come your way. Success comes only through your own initiative.

2 Your ambitions may be thwarted by your own self-centred interests—be thoughtful and considerate of others. Journeys are indicated.

3 If minor worries of a domestic nature are threatened confront them calmly. Beware of secret enemies.

4 Good fortune will attend new business deals. Avoid entering into legal arguments.

5 Contracts and agreements will benefit you financially. A romance may blossom from a friendship.

6 New associations will aid your progress but guard against making rash speculations.

7 You may experience a rise in social position. Secret enemies will seek to do you harm.

8 If your affairs suffer a slight set back, concentrate on one thing at a time and all will be resolved.

9 Travel and sudden changes of plans may seem alarming but are good experience for the future. Good fortune in business awaits you.

10 A new relationship will greatly influence your future, but do not allow this new person to dominate you.

11 Your will be active in

business and in social events—enjoy it but allow some time to relax.

12 You may experience a disappointment in love. Do not allow your unhappiness to cloud the rest of your friendships.

13 Do not allow thrift to develop into avarice and selfishness. Disputes with relations may occur.

14 Take care when making investments. Domestic affairs will progress smoothly.

15 Danger from slander is threatened. Profit from an unexpected source is shown.

16 Curb your desire to spend extravagantly on things that you neither need nor really want.

17 Affairs of the heart will trouble you. Business dealings will prove fortunate.

18 Trivial misunderstandings will cause you stress. A change in lifestyle may also leave you feeling vulnerable.

19 Take care not to let your ambition cloud your judgement. Beware of a business rival.

20 Needless worries connected with domestic affairs will bring unhappiness. Allow a friend to assist you.

21 There will be progress where new ventures will be brought to completion if you are dedicated.

22 Listen to the advice of your elders. Success will attend your endeavours in business.

23 Good fortune will result from an important interview. A love affair may bring you more grief than joy.

24 Adverse criticism will cloud your happiness but believe in yourself and do what you believe to be right.

25 You may have to go on many short journeys. Beware of the flattery of false friends.

26 Social progress will be made, but there are likely to be worries connected with family and friends.

27 A new friendship will

help you on the road to success. Avoid legal disputes.

28 You may be involved with work associated with social reform. Do not be too capricious in business.

29 Dishonest companions threaten your wellbeing. Beware of slanderous tongues.

30 Better times lie ahead for you. Exercise care and thought in the decisions you make.

31 A stranger will bring you good news. Do not neglect your friends and family as they will give you support.

February

1 Seize a coming opportunity in business, you will be fortunate. A change of residence is indicated.

2 A love affair will begin but let your head rule your heart. You must avoid being carried away by emotion.

3 For those who earn their living by the pen it is likely that there will be good fortune. A journey abroad is imminent.

4 You will receive a rebuke, for your own good. Beware of a newly formed friendship.

5 Prosperity lies ahead; do not be overcautious. You may have cause for jealousy in love.

6 Help from friends is indicated. An old love-affair will be renewed; be sure that it is not an attempt to live in the past.

7 You have the desire to travel, but you must not ignore your responsibilities to people at home.

8 Your emotions may cause you misery; control them. A true friend will make themselves known; be sure to recognise this.

9 An important career move will be offered to you. A family quarrel is likely.

10 Petty jealousies may frustrate you. You will shine at social functions.

11 Those who are single will make romantic attachments. The married will receive good news.

12 Avoid lending money. Deception by one of the opposite sex is shown.

13 Much happiness will come to you. You will meet a long-forgotten friend.

14 A journey and a loss are foretold. A good opportunity will arise in business.

15 You will be deeply concerned with love affairs. Take the advice of your elders.

16 You must devote less time to pleasure. Hard work will be met with reward.

17 A great temptation is threatened. A friend's good influence will aid you.

18 A pleasant journey. Prosperity will result from a business conference.

19 Jealous persons will seek to harm you. Avoid quarrelling, especially at home.

20 Some secret matter will be made known to you. You can profit by it.

21 Beware of an argument with an elder person. You will make some important new friends.

22 Beware of helping unworthy causes. You will feel the need of spiritual enlightenment.

23 Good fortune will attend courtships. Married people will feel the bond between them and their partners stengthen.

24 The routine of your life will change unexpectedly. This is the chance to show your talents.

25 You will find spiritual peace and success in your work. Relationships may prove more problematic.

26 Restlessness and emotional romances are indicated for the young. Older persons will prosper considerably.

27 Be careful about how you speak and write about others. A profitable deal is indicated.

28 A new venture will succeed. Much domestic happiness and contentment is promised.

29 Affairs of the heart will occupy your mind, but

do not neglect the more tedious matters of work and finance.

March

1 New friendships will be formed. Good fortune will attend your business ventures.

2 Your hopes of success will be realized. Beware of risky investments.

3 Misunderstandings will occur with those you love. An important domestic change is foreshadowed.

4 Avoid contact with lawyers. A bright and interesting social life will keep you on your toes.

5 You will not be without vexations and worries. Vital changes will occur that are for the best.

6 Some difficult situations lie in store. New friendships and useful associations will soon be formed.

7 Business and investments will prosper. Journeys and changes of occupation are indicated.

8 You will be called upon

to make a sacrifice. A letter of great importance will reach you.

9 Prosperity in love affairs. Your work and business dealings will improve.

10 Accept the aid that a friend will offer. Travel is likely, bringing with it good fortune.

11 Great happiness and success lies ahead of you. Avoid petty arguments and domestic disruption.

12 Loss of personal belongings is shown. Curb extravagance and ignore advice of false friends.

13 An exciting and interesting social life lies ahead. However, do not enter into new ventures recklessly.

14 New and loyal friendships will be made. Love affairs will receive a temporary setback.

15 Someone will seek to influence you wrongly. You will make headway in your profession.

16 A change of career may take you abroad or give you a different lifestyle.

Success will crown your efforts.

17 You will obtain your desires. Money will come to you from an unexpected source.

18 You have excellent prspects, be sure to take advantage of them. There will be changes in your affairs.

19 Strife and contention are shown. Business will prosper and new ventures will be entered upon.

20 An old friend will seek to help you. A long journey is promised.

21 A romantic attachment will be formed. Financial improvement will leave you feeling more secure.

22 Place a curb on your rashness and avoid extravagance. Sincere friends will offer help.

23 Great changes and a new way of life are shown. Take care not to neglect and lose your old friends.

24 Sporting activities should bring you suc-

cess—either in attaining fitness or through an award. Expect a great opportunity to arise shortly.

25 Love affairs approach a crisis. Beware of slanderous tongues who seek to harm you.

26 Be careful of specious offers. Work hard, for a generous reward is indicated

27 You are likely to achieve great good fortune. A friend will need your aid—do not disappoint them.

28 You will be called upon to make sacrifices. These will mark a turning point in your life for the better.

29 Look after your health as you may suffer a minor illness. Domestic affairs will undergo a distinct change.

30 Legal matters will arise, a legacy being the reason. Your progress in your career will be slow but definitely sure.

31 Good friends will seek to help you. A journey

abroad will be undertaken.

April

1 Financial prospects will steadily improve. Important news will be received from abroad.

2 Take every opportunity that presents itself. Your determination means that excellent progress lies ahead.

3 Do not place too much faith in friendships and new acquaintances; you may be deceived by someone you thought you could trust.

4 Be very cautious if embarking upon any new enterprises. Exercise extra caution in money matters.

5 Bad news may be received by letter. Avoid starting upon a long journey.

6 You are likely to experience good fortune with regard to money but do not make any rash investments. Be more self-confident and others will have more faith in you.

7 Exercise restraint and avoid temptation and scandal. You will enter into many important business negotiations.

8 Much correspondence in relation to business matters is indicated. Listen to friendly advice, which will be of value.

9 You will experience many changes, mostly in the areas of love, money and domestic affairs. These may cause you stress.

10 Take great care with your finances as you may have money worries. Do not gossip about a trusted friend or you will surely lose them.

11 Your prospects are excellent—have faith in yourself and do what you can to ensure that the happiness you deserve is realised.

12 Listen to any friendly advice that is offered. Your problems could be solved by the objective opinion of someone who is not involved.

13 You may experience an

illness of some kind. Look after yourself and your health and your fortune will improve.

14 You may experience success in a sporting activity or outdoor pursuit. Financial success is predicted.

15 You will make new friends and lose old ones. A journey may lead to a consequent change of career.

16 You may experience difficulties, especially in business. Sacrifices will be called for.

17 Pay attention to details—both in finance and in personal relationships—otherwise you may suffer delays and disappointments.

18 Improved conditions, but concentrated effort is necessary. You may experience much improved financial security.

19 A period of minor misfortunes, followed by improved circumstances and new companionships.

20 A new sphere of life is shown. A change of career will bring you financial gain.

21 Make some real decisions about a change of direction that is badly needed. Making assumptions without knowing the facts will be disastrous.

22 You will be sorely vexed by a relative but learn to curb your temper as they do not mean to be the source of such stress for you.

23 A friend may experience an illness for which they will need your support. Your help is vital for them and will bring you good fortune.

24 Domestic relationships may be strained so work hard to avoid this. Worry and distress will be tempered by some good news.

25 Avoid making an impulsive change of occupation; your present circumstances will soon improve.

26 You will experience some inevitable disap-

pointments. Be patient and you will see that they make way for other better opportunities

27 There will be a considerable addition to financial resources. You may have to travel abroad due to your career.

28 Danger lies ahead, but it may be avoided if discretion is exercised in friendships. Do not take your friends for granted.

29 Risky financial ventures should be avoided. Work hard and play it safe

30 News of a mixed character will reach you. You will experience varying fortune in love and business.

May

1 Beware of giving way to your desires. You will find joy in a harmonious friendship.

2 Many exciting journeys are ahead. An increase of work will be tiring but it will lead to prosperity.

3 Someone will attempt to interfere in your life who has no right to do so.

There may be domestic troubles.

4 You are headstrong and inclined not to listen to others, take heed of a friend's advice in a matter over which there is some doubt.

5 Changes of situation may leave you feeling insecure. Beware if you are tempted to deceive a friend—it will lead to disaster.

6 Your ambition will be partly realized but beware of being overconfident and arrogant.

7 You are secretly loved; use your discretion to find by whom. Happiness will follow.

8 Dishonest strangers threaten your business. Speculation will bring losses—be cautious.

9 You are contemplating making an important decision that may cause strife. Take the advice of a relative.

10 Your persistence and willpower will bring you money. Love affairs will prosper.

11 Some gossip will be spread by a false friend. A woman will prove a benefactor.

12 Gaiety and social pleasures are foretold. Delays will occur in business that will prove to be very tiresome.

13 Worry concerning a relative is probable. Gain of money is shown.

14 You may influence a friend for his good. Surprising news from abroad is foreshadowed.

15 You will experience adventurous undertakings, quick courtship, travel and legal business.

16 Success for those in trade. Powerful friends will bring prosperity.

17 Many changes connected with private affairs will occur. Prudence and diplomacy are necessary.

18 Your fortune will depend on your ability. Do not trust to luck.

19 Pleasure rather than work is in store. There may be factors that create unfavourable circumstances for travel.

20 New employment is indicated. A supposed enemy will prove to be a friend.

21 A solution to certain perplexing matters will be found. Success in sport is indicated.

22 Your craving for a change will be satisfied. Many new friends will be made.

23 Money will be received from a source other than your business. Slight illness is predicted.

24 You will be a victim of circumstance. Comfort will be found in a person of the opposite sex.

25 Those in love will achieve their desire. Take care not to let arrogance blind you to the good points of a potential partner

26 A journey abroad is foreshadowed. Friends will be lost and made.

27 Your hot-headedness may lead to disaster. The advice of a friend will prove invaluable.

28 Try not to let your social life stagnate. Avoid gambling and cultivate new acquaintanceships.

29 Discretion will be needed in personal affairs. Avoid the interference of relatives.

30 Let patience control your ambition, and you will make slow but solid progress.

31 You will attend many business meetings and conferences. Love affairs will prove stormy.

June

1 Money from two professions is shown. Be warned against being too extravagant.

2 You may experience temporary setbacks in business. Domestic affairs will be harmonious.

3 Do not undertake any risky business ventures. Work hard and your efforts will be rewarded.

4 An important contract will be signed. A love affair will progress into a courtship

5 Avoid mental overwork.

Beware of the jealousy of business associates, who could harm you

6 Good fortune will attend you. Do not take unnecessary risks with your health.

7 Gossip may affect your life adversely; either about you or produced by you. Avoid it at all costs.

8 Doubt affecting the course of a love affair will disappear. Financial gain is shown.

9 Favours will be received from friends. An agreement or contract is foretold.

10 Your keen judgment will bring you rich reward. New friends will be met.

11 You will experience many ups and downs. Success will come through endeavour.

12 Good luck will be experienced in business. A quarrel with a friend is indicated.

13 Great happiness in domestic affairs is foreshadowed. Important news will be received by post.

14 A lucky business partnership awaits you. New friendships will mean social changes.

15 A change of residence is foretold. News from abroad will affect your career.

16 Restlessness and discontentment mar your progress. Cultivate the power of concentration.

17 New ventures will be successful. A gift of money from a relative is shown.

18 You may receive news of a long lost friend. Pay attention to details at work.

19 Many minor domestic worries beset your path. Your financial status will gradually improve.

20 A journey will materially affect your fortunes. A love affair will come to nothing.

21 The sun of contentment will shine upon you. Lucky speculations are indicated.

22 Keen endeavour will bring you great success. You will receive a small inheritance.

23 Swift developments in business are foreshadowed. Domestic discord will cause periods of unhappiness.

24 Success in financial undertakings is shown. Many new business contracts will be made.

25 You may experience a period of difficulty about which you must not allow yourself to get depressed. This period will pass.

26 Authors and journalists are likely to be successful. New contracts will be signed.

27 A new friendship will materially aid your progress. Beware of injury through idle gossip.

28 Look well ahead before you commit yourself to new responsibilities. A monetary loss is foreshadowed.

29 Love affairs could possibly cause serious complications. Money will be gained through investment.

30 Do not let your heart rule your head. Business

conditions might prove unstable.

July

1 You may have a change of residence, possibly to the country. New interests will arise.

2 A message will reach you from an unexpected source. Troubles will arise.

3 Peace and happiness will rule your spiritual life. Love affairs will prosper.

4 Much worry and the probable break-up of a friendship. A journey to a distant part.

5 True love will enter your life. Your mental horizon will widen.

6 A business proposition will be put to you. A visit to the country is shown.

7 A religious crisis is approached. A period of unease will be followed by great happiness.

8 Young people will prosper in all occupations concerning the arts. Important changes are shown.

9 You will visit many strange places. A new phase of life will be entered upon.

10 Intuition regarding a close friend will prove correct. An interesting discovery will be made.

11 Domestic troubles are foreshadowed. A new source of income will be discovered.

12 Any festivities will take place under your roof. Difficulties will be solved satisfactorily.

13 Success on the stage. Business will prosper, and influential contacts be established.

14 Changes will take place which will be for the better. Short journeys are indicated.

15 You will be required to extend hospitality to a stranger. Social activity and success is promised.

16 Serious disturbances will occur in the home circle. Travels abroad and good news.

17 An unintentional wrong will be done to you. Misunderstandings will

arise, but reconciliation will be effected.

18 A public performance will bring unexpected praise. A period of prosperity lies ahead.

19 You will be called upon to adapt yourself to altered conditions. Much activity is foreshadowed.

20 New friends and the beginnings of a love affair are in store. Beware of scandals.

21 Success is indicated for those engaged in mental work. A death will bring a change of environment.

22 Increasingly you will be acting for the good of others. An important contract will be entered into.

23 You will successfully undertake a difficult piece of work. Some worry is shown.

24 Any new contacts will be made. You will be enabled to do a great service.

25 You will have concerns over money matters that will create difficulties within your family.

26 Others will be inclined to impose upon you. Guard against malice and ill-health.

27 A journey will be undertaken on behalf of a friend. The death of a relative is shown.

28 Those engaged in legal, accountancy and research work will achieve success..

29 You will make a momentous decision. A change of occupation will be delayed by a short illness.

30 Many opportunities will occur to achieve recognition. Financial gain and some minor disturbances.

31 Some unpleasant gossip, but an old quarrel is made up. Marriage is shown.

August

1 Rebuffs will be met with, but they will be of little consequence. News of money.

2 Expansion of business and corresponding increase in income. A love affair is shown.

3　Travel brings both pleasure and troubles. Homecoming will bring renewed happiness.

4　You will have to work hard but this will eventually be rewarded through the approval of others.

5　Realization of cherished desires, brought about by a change of occupation. You will make several new friends.

6　Do not allow yourself to become anxious and stressed by the careless actions of others because this may affect your health adversely.

7　Pay attention to your family duties which you may neglect for selfish reasons.

8　You may suffer due to an unrequited love and be disappointed regarding a career goal. You will make some new friends.

9　You have many plans but may be putting them off until you think the time is suitable—the time is now.

10　Hard work will be rewarded with success and profit, but do not neglect the other aspects of your life.

11　Your health may suffer so take extra care over health and fitness. Pay attention to your diet in particular.

12　There will be luck in many ventures undertaken, but a danger of failure in some unless care is exercised.

13　There may be expansion of business and increased return for labours.

14　A meeting with fresh faces, several experiences and some absence from home.

15　There will be good news from absent friends, bringing an offer to join them in their prosperous activities.

16　You will eventually achieve inner peace after some disappointment and worries.

17　Travel may feature strongly in your life with a joyful homecoming.

18　You will receive a strange proposition, and a refusal to take part in it is imperative.

19 Refuse any requests to undertake public duties which you feel are too much responsibility.

20 Progress in love affairs, but a temporary setback in career pursuits. Signs of money scarcity.

21 You will be especially active in both business and sport. Success is indicated in both spheres.

22 A visit to a strange land, with at least one exciting adventure. Changes in domestic life.

23 You will achieve a slight improvement in financial status but you must still be frugal with your money.

24 You are naturally optimistic person and must not allow the actions and moods of others to change this.

25 Seek to make new friends and start new endeavours or your life may become monotonous.

26 Letters are an important feature in your life and you may receive fortunate news from one very soon.

27 Quarrels and misunderstandings. Avoid arguments and pay no heed to slander.

28 Improvement in your career will lead to improvement in your life in general.

29 Indiscretions will lead to the breaking of associations. Misunderstandings will eventually be explained.

30 You have been feeling neglected, and not appreciated in the way you deserve, you must make these feelings known for others to change their behaviour accordingly.

31 Be very wary of risky business ventures and strange propositions from people you do not know well enough.

September

1 Beware of having a too materialistic outlook. Money is likely to become more important then people.

2 You are allowing your intellect to go to waste because you are not living up to your full potential.

3 Trying irritations are in store. Promise of great improvement in business is shown.

4 You love romance and adventure but it will not come to you if you sit back and wait for it!

5 Much prosperity for those connected with industry. Young people will form deep attachments.

6 A better position will be offered you. A family reunion is likely to occur.

7 Festivity, petty quarrels, and new friends are shown. There are signs of temporary ill-health.

8 A disappointment in love is foretold. You will find a new happiness.

9 Resist the urge to argue with a female relative; it will only end in bitterness and regret

10 You should pursue your present plans without fear. Beware of a plausible stranger.

11 Luck will attend an investment. A difficulty in a love affair will end happily.

12 You will meet a new and influential friend. Speculation should be avoided.

13 If your financial position has been worrying in the past you will find yourself in a position where it is strengthened.

14 Great changes are in store. New attachments will be made and finances increased.

15 Minor disappointments will occur. Beware of a deception by a friend.

16 Your life is likely to be filled with romance and devotion. Pleasant surprises await disappointed lovers.

17 You will be helped by your friends. Your work will attract the attention of influential persons.

18 Sorrow may come for a while; but a new happiness will enter your life.

19 You have very high ideals when it comes to romance—these may be too high for anyone else to live up to.

20 A surprising occurrence will result in a gain. Curb a tendency towards extravagance.

21 Profit from investments is indicated. Complicated love affairs may cause confusion.

22 Much correspondence over private matters. Change of position will bring prosperity.

23 Petty jealousies among your friends are likely. Do not neglect your closest friends for new acquaintances.

24 Hard work will bring reward and romance will enter your life almost without you even realising it.

25 Business may increase, but at the expense of friendship. Avoid avarice.

26 If you are thinking of changing your life or ending a relationship on a whim, take time to think before you make any such rash action.

27 Allow friends to give you advice and listen to them. You will have an important decision to make.

28 Sorrow will reign for a time, but joy and prosperity will follow in due time.

29 Beware of a scheming stranger. By work and discretion you will find success.

30 A friend is likely to become a romantic interest for you—prepare to be swept off your feet!

October

1 Exercise prudence in regard to health and wealth. Danger from unexpected sources is predicted.

2 You have a determined personality and must realise that you are capable of achieving your goals.

3 Self-indulgence will mar your progress. Do not become associated with questionable schemes.

4 A quarrel with a friend will cause you unhappiness. Guard your quick temper.

5 A change of residence is

very likely. You will hear some good news from abroad.

6 A stroke of good fortune awaits you. Many pleasurable excursions are indicated.

7 You will be blessed with romance and affection, be sure to give as well as receive. Financial affairs will prosper.

8 Travel and new undertakings are in store for you. Avoid domestic quarrels.

9 Business ventures are likely to be successful, but do not take unnecessary risks.

10 Look well before you leap. Your life will be marked by many upheavals.

11 New friendships will aid your success and bring you much happiness.

12 Do not be over-rash in your speculations. A temporary financial reverse is indicated.

13 Endeavour to live within your means. Overindulgence in luxury is shown.

14 Seize all opportunities

that come your way and you are bound to succeed.

16 A relation will cause discord in your family circle. Do not listen to malicious gossips.

17 Through sharp words you will lose a friendship. Curb your argumentative nature and try to control your temper.

18 New friendships will lead to new projects. Financial success is predicted.

19 A journey will be embarked upon. A reunion of friends is indicated.

20 An unexpected financial gain is foretold. You will make a new friend.

21 Disappointment followed by a pleasant surprise is presaged. A change of residence will be made.

22 Be cautious in money affairs. You will end your business and increase your prestige.

23 Success will reward your efforts. A turbulent love affair is near at hand.

24 You will be blessed with unexpected good for-

tune. Beware of a plausible stranger.

25 A change of occupation is predicted. A jealous woman may cause family quarrels.

26 Social functions and entertainments will be abundant. A misunderstanding with a friend is likely.

27 Take heed of the advice of an elder. Extravagance on your part will cause great worry.

28 Many new friends will be made. You will prosper by a change of occupation.

29 Hard work, with good reward, lies ahead. Family quarrels are shown.

30 You will meet an influential stranger. Good news concerning domestic matters is presaged.

31 You have many fortunate events in store. Material and spiritual gains are strongly indicated.

November

1 A friend will betray you. A secret will be discovered and new associations found.

2 Do not neglect your close relationships for fickle associations.

3 Strangers will cause you to lose money. Help from relatives and a long journey will result.

4 Mistaken ideas will cause difficulties and misunderstandings. A new start in life will be made.

5 You will be tempted to betray a trust, but will not do so. Friendships and private interests prosper.

6 Beware of unwise extravagance, followed by a period of recuperation.

7 Some new acquaintances will prove worthless. An opportunity of change will bring happiness.

8 Business affairs will suffer a serious reverse. Greater independence will bring financial stability.

9 A relative will seek your assistance, but others will attempt to influence you wrongly.

10 You will meet someone who will greatly influence your life. A successful lawsuit is shown.

11 Hard work will meet with success in business. A long and pleasant holiday will be enjoyed.

12 Social recognition awaits you. The opportunity to enter upon a public career will occur.

13 Both love and respect will be yours. An unexpected gift will lead to some travel.

14 A greatly-prized friendship will threaten your schemes. Some financial loss will occur, but happiness in love.

15 Your present enterprise will be successfully concluded. Much vigilance is necessary. Beware of tricksters

16 An important public gathering will take place. A momentous event will bring release from worry.

17 An unexpected legacy will bring great opportunities. Beware of theft. Love affairs prosper.

18 Success and popularity will offer temptation. A wrong decision will be followed by some difficulty.

19 A chance meeting will strongly influence your life. A legal agreement is signed.

20 Foolish people will attempt to lead you astray. An unpleasant situation develops, but your success is assured.

21 Your ambitions may be realized. Changes of residence will bring a new interest.

22 Your obstinacy will prove a pitfall. An eventful time will bring both joy and sorrow.

23 Luck in speculation will favour you. Excesses will nearly lead to disaster, which is just averted.

24 Temporary estrangement caused through your overbearing manner. A period of unrest, followed by a pleasant surprise.

25 An opportunity to make money will be given to you. You must be pre-

pared for a lot of ups and downs.

26 An unwise remark will make an enemy. Events will, however, favour you in the end.

27 Do not be discouraged if your luck runs out. This is a temporary setbacks and determination will win through.

28 A promising love affair will suffer a setback. Advice from a friend will aid you. Business prospers.

29 Fortune and happiness await you. A new source of income is found. Avoid recklessness.

30 An illness caused through your own carelessness will not prove dangerous. A business relationship is broken.

December

1 Be humble enough to listen to the advice of a friend. By your work you will gain recognition.

2 Affairs of the heart may be stormy. A distant relative will bring you good fortune.

3 Exercise caution in your actions. An enemy will endeavour to deceive you.

4 Harmonious family life is presaged. Seek further afield for business success.

5 New enterprise, new friends, and a new residence will be welcome changes but necessarily stressful ones.

6 A young person will cause you anxiety. Slight monetary gains are indicated.

7 Cultivate your intellect, it will bring you success. Avoid passionate love affairs.

8 Success will be gained in a new sphere. A change of residence is possible.

9 Annoyance by relatives will be experienced. Strangers will bring unexpected gains.

10 Be on your guard against someone from a foreign country. A slight loss of money is foretold.

11 Your plans will succeed. A faithful friend will be

found. A journey is probable.

12 A loss will bring unexpected happiness. A great improvement in health is likely.

13 Good fortune will result from hard work and enterprise.

14 Good news awaits you. Business will prosper. A long cherished wish will be fulfilled.

15 New schemes promise success. A quarrel with an old friend may occur.

16 An unfortunate legal dispute threatens you. A loved one will bring you comfort and happiness.

17 Social functions will occupy much time. Your work may suffer through neglect.

18 Your social life will improve and a close relationship will blossom into love.

19 You have a lot of hard work ahead of you. A former enemy will prove a new-found friend.

20 Your foresight will bring reward. A position of note awaits you.

21 An old friendship will be revived. Much travel and adventure are foretold.

22 Jealousy will bring distress. Take care that you do not lose a friend through a misjudgement

23 Good news from a relative. A quarrel with a loved one and a journey abroad are presaged.

24 Happiness and harmony will attend you. The single are likely to find love.

25 Peace, progress, and spiritual benefits will be yours. You have a fortunate future.

26 A senseless quarrel will put a friendship at risk. Avoid this by controlling your temper and showing restraint.

27 A friend will bring you comfort and happiness in a difficult time.

28 Good fortune through a lucky speculation is predicted. A visit abroad is probable.

29 One of your ambitions will be realized. There is also a disappointment in store.

30 An increase of wealth and a change of residence are foretold. Love affairs will run smoothly.

31 You will have an important decision to make. Success may come very soon.